Entering The Global Engineering Market
A Correlational Study of Cultural Intelligence and Market Orientation

Dr. Stephen R. Galati

Copyright © 2016 Stephen R. Galati

All rights reserved.

ISBN: 1545387540
ISBN-13: 978-1545387542

ENTERING THE GLOBAL ENGINEERING MARKET: A CORRELATIONAL

STUDY OF CULTURAL INTELLIGENCE AND MARKET ORIENTATION

by

Stephen R. Galati

Copyright 2015

A Dissertation Presented in Partial Fulfillment
of the Requirements for the Degree
Doctor of Management in Organizational Leadership

University of Phoenix

The Dissertation Committee for Stephen R. Galati certifies approval of the following dissertation:

ENTERING THE GLOBAL ENGINEERING MARKET: A

CORRELATIONAL STUDY OF CULTURAL INTELLIGENCE AND

MARKET ORIENTATION

Committee: Debbie Ritter-Williams, PhD, Chair

John Peed, DA, Committee Member

Lionel De Souza, PhD, Committee Member

Debbie Ritter-Williams, PhD
Debbie Ritter-Williams

John H. Peed
John Peed

Lionel de Souza
Lionel De Souza

Jeremy Moreland
Jeremy Moreland, PhD
Academic Dean, School of Advanced Studies
University of Phoenix

Date Approved: December 15, 2015

ABSTRACT

Faced with increasing domestic competition from non-U.S. firms and a growing global marketplace, U.S.-based engineering firms have turned their focus to globalizing their services. Understanding the multifaceted cultural aspects of marketing and penetrating the global engineering market requires heightened cross-cultural leadership competencies in tandem with a strategic market orienting activities. The purpose of this quantitative correlational study was to determine any relationship that may exist between the variables of cultural intelligence and market orientation of decision makers at U.S.-based engineering firms to the dependent variable of entering the global marketplace. Participants were composed of senior-level global engineering and marketing decision makers from U.S.-based engineering firms listed on ENR's Top Global and International Design Firms listings. The study included an online survey consisting of the Cultural Intelligence Scale and the individual market orientation scale, the I-MARKOR instrument. Statistical correlational analysis of the collected data indicated some positive relationships between factors of cultural intelligence and global market orientation. The analysis indicated a significant relationship exists between the aggregates of cultural intelligence and global market orientation. The study conclusions should assist globally-focused engineering firms to better penetrate the worldwide marketplace and to recognize the benefits of cultural intelligence and global market orientation leadership skillsets. Since there was a significant relationship between cultural intelligence and individual market orientation, global-looking domestic engineering firms are encouraged to invest deeper in enhancing the factors that comprise cultural intelligent leadership decisions in the organization. The recommendations presented in the research study outline suggestions for future research and practice. .

DEDICATION

I dedicate this dissertation to my wife, Janet, and my five children, Zachary, Nicholas, Sarah, Jacob, and Emily. They have encouraged me throughout my whole doctoral journey and continue to inspire me with their unwavering love and support. Without them, this work and the fulfillment of a life goal, would not have been possible. I could only hope to show my children this same support as they find interesting and inventive ways to exercise their intellect, or as they call it, their "smarticles"..

CONTENTS

	Acknowledgments	i
1	Introduction	1
2	Literature Review	18
3	Research Methodology	53
4	Results	69
5	Conclusions and Recommendations	113
	References	131

A	Informed Consent Form	146
B	SurveyMonkey Permission	149
C	Permission to use Existing Surveys	153
D	Survey Instruments	156
E	Demographic Survey	160
F	Participant Engagement Email	163
G	Confidentiality Agreement	167

ACKNOWLEDGMENTS

First, I want to express interminable gratitude to my mentor, Dr. Debbie Ritter-Williams, who stuck with me through the good and bad times, and who always found ways to gently guide me forward. Dr. Deb is a remarkable mentor and scholar, who, through our years of work together, has showed me what it means to be a diligent, patient, confident, and encouraging academic. Her professionalism and high standards ensured the development and production of a quality work. I have met countless intellectuals and scholars throughout my many years of study, from my engineering and English rhetoric programs to my emergency preparedness and management studies. However, Dr. Deb stands alone as my most esteemed and beloved advisor.

I want to thank my committee members, Dr. John Peed and Dr. Lionel De Souza, for their time, support, and many exceptional contributions to my study. I also want to thank Dr. Janice Novello for her review and contributions earlier in my study. My dissertation is a far better work through their guidance, perspectives, and recommendations.

I want to recognize my wonderful Academic Counselors at the University of Phoenix, Carola Garfias and Chris LaPrath, for all of their support, direction, and care throughout my doctoral journey.

Finally, I want to acknowledge those individuals who have supported my doctoral journey and inspired me to complete my dissertation. I must thank my parents for providing me the love and strong academic foundation that have led me to my doctoral degree. I want to acknowledge Drs. Soon Ang, Linn Van Dyne, and Christine Koh for allowing me to use their cultural intelligence scale in this research, and also Dr. Francine Schlosser for allowing me to use her individual market orientation measure. I would also like to thank those who took time out of their busy lives and participated in the study. Lastly, I want to acknowledge my Aunt Eileen, who whole-heartedly supported my doctoral journey and would frequently call me to inquire about my studies, offer her steadfast encouragement, and let me know she was proud of me. Unfortunately, my Aunt passed away before she could see these words; however, I will always remember her reassurance, love, and support.

ONE

INTRODUCTION

United States (U.S.)-based engineering firms are pushed by increasing competition to bring their once domestically sold engineering services internationally and become global providers (Acosta, Leon, Conrad, & Malave, 2010; Scholte, 2005). Meeting the demands of the global market requires these organizations not only to provide exceptional engineering services in foreign territory but also to understand and become oriented to the cultures and customs within these new service areas (Acosta et al., 2010; Marber, 2009; Valenti, 1995; Vieth & Smith, 2008; Yip, 2003). While some engineering firms meet success, other firms do not and fail to transition from a domestic marketplace to a global one. IBISWorld Inc. (2012) stated engineering firms that remain sustainable and successfully profitable widen their service range and embrace emerging and global markets. Understanding the multifaceted cultural aspects of marketing and penetrating the global engineering market affects organizational decision making, sales and client purchasing behaviors, operational process, and service products (Acosta et al., 2010; de Mooij, 2010). Cultural issues and market orientation differences can pose challenges for leaders of U.S.-based engineering firms trying to transition and win work in the vast global economy (Hansen, Tanuja, Weilbaker, & Guesalaga, 2011).

Cultural Intelligence (known as CQ) is a model designed to distinguish an individual's ability to adapt to unfamiliar cultural environments (Ang & Van Dyne, 2008). Cultural intelligence blends four distinct components of an individual's cultural understanding, namely cognitive, metacognitive, behavioral, and motivational elements (Earley & Ang, 2003; Livermore, 2010; Mannor, 2008). Globally-focused organizations engage staff cultural intelligence competencies to identify cultural differences, heighten the organization's cross-cultural perspective, and transition into foreign cultural environments (Livermore, 2010; Ward & Fischer, 2008). Likewise, globally-focused engineering firms from the United States require cultural competency and individual market knowledge to gain entrance into foreign markets (Pearl, 2007, 2009; Valenti, 1995). Culturally intelligent individuals offer value as cultural adaptors and cultural leaders within their organizations to enter global engineering markets and capture project work.

U.S.-based engineering firms have also met global success through market orientation (known as MO), a traditional construct that involves the organizational development of market information regarding client needs and customs, the sharing of this information within the organization, and the organization's use of this information within the market (Kohli, Jaworski, & Kumar, 1993). Business performance, domestic or globally, is dependent upon market orientation and that better targeted and developed market orientation will increase business performance (Narver & Slater, 1990). Naturally, organizations engage global market orientation through intelligence-rich penetration strategies and market business plans. In fact, Kohli and Jaworski (1990) advanced this idea, defining market orientation as a mix of intelligence generation, intelligence dissemination, and responsiveness. Schlosser (2004) realigned this definition of market orientation from a firm-level concept to an individual level capability, revising the three-component model to information acquisition, information sharing, and strategic response. Schlosser's (2004) revised model complements the market activities of service firms by taking into account the individual contributions regarding market orientation (Schlosser & McNaughton, 2009). This model parallels the cultural and business elements involved with globalizing an engineering firm because it enables a bottom-up perspective to these cultural and business elements as well as the organization's market orientation activities.

Leaders and decision makers at domestic engineering firms looking for successful entry and new work in the global market need to understand different market cultures, expectations of those cultures, and ways to orient themselves with these new markets (Bueno & Tubbs, 2004; Robinson & Harvey, 2008). Ultimately, these *decision makers* – those who make strategic decisions about services, products, and marketplace activities for a firm – require individual cultural intelligence and global market orientation skills to support their company's collective informed decisions regarding entry into the global marketplace (Hansen, Tanuja, Weilbaker, & Guesalaga, 2011; Livermore, 2010). *Entry* into the global market is distinguished within the study as the act of domestic firms validly acknowledging, pursuing, transforming for, and eventually winning work in a non-U.S. market. Market entry involves capturing global market space through a single project or multiple projects. For comparison, the lowest ranking U.S.-based firm in Engineering News Record's (ENR) 2012 Top 150 Global Design Firm listing (ranked 149 out of 150) had $164.0 million in total revenue and only $2.5 million in non-U.S. revenue (McGraw-Hill Companies, 2012). Chapter 1 contains an overview of the study's background of the problem, statement of the problem, purpose, leadership significance, and nature of the study. The chapter continues with the study's research question and hypotheses, and concludes with the study's conceptual framework, definitions, assumptions, scope, limitations, and delimitations.

Background of the Problem

The engineering market landscape has grown over the past decades from providing services domestically within the U.S. to providing services globally. The global director of business development and planning at CH2M Hill, a U.S.-based engineering firm that has achieved unprecedented success overseas, suggested that the growth rate of the U.S. marketplace has been dwarfed by the faster growing non-U.S. market (Buckley, 2010). Leaders at domestic engineering firms are facing an influx of foreign competitors on their home turf and have been forced to search for opportunities outside the country to meet their internal business demands as well as their external engineering market challenges. With tougher domestic competition, U.S.-based engineering firms are looking toward the global market for organizational growth and sustainability (Culbert, 2011; Marber, 2009; Yip, 2003). Domestic engineering firms without a substantive in-country niche have turned to the globalization of services (Knab, 2008; Scholte, 2005).

With such an immediate push to globalize services, U.S.-based engineering firms of all sizes have confronted the various international challenges of the engineering marketplace. The leadership activities related to globalization have implications for firm size and the characteristics of business, such as competition, market boundaries, and staffing "centers of gravity" (Prahalad, 1997, p. 160-161). An example of these implications is the trend in the global market for leaders to deliver design and construct contracts, which unquestionably favors larger engineering firms that not only have the requisite experienced design and construction staff in-house but also have the business mechanisms in-place to deliver such a contract (IBISWorld Inc., 2010). Livermore (2010) added that "leadership today is a multicultural challenge" (p. 3). Unfortunately, U.S. organizations that have little exposure to global business environments are ill-prepared for a true global presence (National Institute of Standards and Technology, 2000; Ng, Tan, & Ang, 2011). Leaders from other domestic engineering firms have learned to meet these globalization challenges and discover pathways to enter and succeed in the global marketplace. Successful global firms have recognized the cross-culture competencies needed for global success, including cultural intelligence and cross-cultural leadership (Livermore, 2010; Valenti, 1995; Vieth & Smith, 2008).

Cultural intelligence has begun surfacing as a formidable indicator of a leader's cross-cultural competencies. Faced with unfamiliar cultural environments and business customs, culturally intelligent leaders can offer inherent value as their organizations enter global engineering markets and attempt to capture overseas project work. Such manifestations include the ability to identify cultural differences, heighten the organization's cross-cultural perspective, and facilitate transition of the organization into foreign cultural environments (Livermore, 2010; Ward & Fischer, 2008). Leadership contributions to an organizational cross-cultural perspective are often varied depending upon individual leader understandings, organizational investments, and the cumulative perspective of the top management team. Cultural intelligence involves recognizing the cultural subtleties of the target market and understanding the abilities within the firm pursuing work in that target market.

Similar to the variation in culturally intelligent leadership choices is the variance between marketing engineering services in the domestic market and the global market. In the domestic market, there exist local subtleties to the marketing message that support an overall consistent approach. In the global market, each target country might expect a specific approach to reach that glocalized market. With such variant requirements in the global marketplace, globalization market approaches need to be multicultural, multi-faceted, complex plans (Hofstede & Hofstede, 2005; Ng, Tan, & Ang, 2011; Scholte, 2005). Specifically, successful marketing approaches on the global front are dependent upon the target market's cultural customs and value systems. Firm leaders need to understand these target market customs and values to deliver a potent marketing message that may be well-received and acceptable (Nakata & Sivakumar, 2001; Tucker, 2000; Yip, 2003). Leaders implementing cross-cultural approaches to marketing and using cultural intelligence in marketing messages can achieve global market orientation, penetration, and success (Cayla & Arnould, 2008; de Mooij, 2010; Matear, 2009; Vytlacil, 2010).

Many large engineering firms have found success overseas with differing cross-cultural and market orientation approaches. Leadership at U.S.-based engineering magnate Fluor Corporation, which is ranked number five in ENR's Top 150 Global Design Firms and number one in ENR's Top 200 International Design Firms listings for 2012, has achieved global success with the ability to recognize the overarching importance of understanding cultures, customs, and politics (McGraw-Hill Companies, 2010, 2012; Valenti, 1995). Los Angeles-based AECOM Technology Corporation, which is ranked number one and number three in ENR's 2010 Global and International Design Firms listings respectively, has found market orientation and cross-cultural success through leveraging regional firm acquisitions (Buckley, 2010; McGraw-Hill Companies, 2010). Both large-scale engineering firms intermixed cross-cultural and market orientation competencies differently, but with the similar result of global market penetration and success.

Domestic engineering firms, like Fluor Corporation and AECOM Technology Corporation, have met success through an organization-specific approach to global market orientation. Global market orientation enables global-focused leaders to develop market intelligence related to the needs and business customs of the non-U.S. market, share global knowledge internally, and respond to these market needs (Kohli, Jaworski, & Kumar, 1993). These documented success stories and necessary market orientation activities are the product of significant fiscal and managerial investments by organizational leadership and top management. Without a strategy for developing global market orientation and cross-cultural competency, U.S.-based engineering firms of all sizes face difficulty and potential failure in understanding and meeting the needs of the global marketplace.

Statement of the Problem

The U.S. engineering industry has experienced an influx of foreign-based engineering firms with a domestic engineering market growing faster than the global engineering marketplace, approximately 8% per year since 2004 (IBISWorld Inc., 2009). The global engineering marketplace has had negative growth since 2006 (-0.4% annually) and is estimated a marginal 3.7% annual growth until 2016 (Culbert, 2011). With nearly half (47.4%) of U.S. patents going to foreign organizations and the top 10 engineering design firms doing work in the U.S. being foreign-based, domestic engineering firms have been forced to pursue global markets (McGraw-Hill Companies, 2009; Plunkett, 2010). The general problem is that with negligible growth and as foreign-based firms capture increasingly more domestic work, U.S.-originated engineering firms are compelled to become globally reaching and offer global engineering services for organizational and service sustainability (Brown, 2009; Culbert, 2011; Fuller, 2004; Vieth & Smith, 2008).

As firms become more globally-focused in their outlook and operations, the necessity to work in and understand diverse cultures intensifies (Wren, 2005). U.S. engineering leaders are witnessing that domestic and global markets are substantially different and that using domestic strategies globally is not sufficient as an approach for market penetration (Alimienė & Kuvykaitė, 2008; Valenti, 1995). The ability to move from domestic strategies to valid global strategies may depend on leadership with global market orientation and an understanding of cultural expectations (Bueno &

Tubbs, 2004; Knab, 2008; Robinson & Harvey, 2008).

The specific problem is that although researchers have suggested that global market orientation must be culturally sensitive to be successful, the specific nature of the relationship between market orientation and cultural intelligence is unknown. The lack of knowledge relative to the relationship between market orientation and cultural intelligence deprives leaders and decision makers of valuable contextual information when determining their desired course of action within global and cross-cultural contexts (Kirca & Hult, 2009). Janssens and Cappellen (2008) added that further study is needed to relate cultural intelligence with different types of global work and with issues associated with winning global work. Advancing this need for understanding, Brettel, Engelen, Heinemann, and Vadhanasindhu (2008) identified culturally sensitive and insensitive relationships between global leader decision making and market orientation in new global ventures. The authors indicated a connection between decision maker cultural behaviors and management applications with market orientation; however, they recommended further study to test relationships between cultural management and market orientation in established companies.

Further study is needed to quantify the relationship between cross-cultural and market orientation competencies in the context of the global engineering arena (Alimienė & Kuvykaitė, 2008; Nakata & Sivakumar, 2001; Valenti, 1995). This quantitative correlational study was conducted through the online surveying of global leaders from U.S.-based engineering firms established and recognized in the global marketplace.

Purpose of the Study

The purpose of this quantitative correlational study was to determine any relationship that may exist between the independent variables of cultural intelligence and market orientation of decision makers at U.S.-based engineering firms to the dependent variable of entering the global marketplace. Participants were composed of a group of senior-level global engineering and marketing decision makers from U.S.-based engineering firms listed on ENR's Top 150 Global Design Firms and Top 200 International Design Firms listings. The participants responded to a survey comprised of items on the multidimensional Cultural Intelligence Scale (CQS) and the Schlosser (2004) I-MARKOR individual market orientation scale.

This research was compatible with a quantitative approach because a quantitative approach allowed the researcher to examine a distinct problem or happening using a sample of a population to discover "associations among different variables" (Cooper & Schindler, 2003, p. 161). Correlational research delineates linearity between multiple variables without designating a definitive cause and effect relationship (Salkind,

2003). A correlational design was the natural choice for this study because the two variables, cultural intelligence and market orientation, have an unknown influence on each other when related to domestic engineering firms competing globally. Correlational research commonly is used to determine the existence of a relationship among two or more variables and assist researchers in predicting outcomes (Salkind, 2003). Given that the relationship between cultural intelligence and market orientation is not thoroughly understood, the correlational design provided statistical validation for or against any influence or relationship.

Nature of the Study

This research study used a quantitative research method as the intent was to understand relationships between cultural intelligence and market orientation within U.S.-based engineering firms aimed at the global marketplace. Quantitative methods help characterize trends or clarify relationships among two or more variables and precisely measure these relationships (Cooper & Schindler, 2003; Johnson & Christensen, 2012). Quantitative methods involve statistical analysis and comparison of numerical or categorical data gathered from any mix of surveys, interviews, observations, and document analyses (Symonds & Gorard, 2010). This study involved a survey based on the Ang et al.'s (2007) Cultural Intelligence Scale and the Schlosser (2004) I-MARKOR individual market orientation scale.

The qualitative research method is exploratory and was not suitable for this study because much was known about each variable of the problem, the phenomenon of these variables was quantifiable, the context of the study was understood, and the study boundaries were well defined (Johnson & Christensen, 2012; Klopper, 2008). Cultural intelligence and market orientation have been studied copiously and each related to various leadership and business variables both on an individual and organizational level. With such a depth of examination already in the body of knowledge, further exploration would be unnecessary. Qualitative methods also involve a high researcher involvement focused on interpreting the phenomenon; however, this study necessitated precise measurement of the variable relationships and limited researcher involvement to avoid any bias (Cooper & Schindler, 2003).

The correlational study had an explanatory design to delineate why cultural intelligence and market orientation affect global-bound U.S. engineering firms. Salkind (2003) and Chen and Popovich (2002) explained that researchers use an explanatory correlational research design to help relate different variables, either on a one-to-one or one-to-many basis. The explanatory design faced market orientation, a variable that has a known link to global engineering firm success, with another variable, cultural intelligence (Neuman, 2006). This design aligned with the study's purpose, namely to determine the relationship between the factors of cultural intelligence and individual market orientation in the context of U.S.-based engineering firms entering the global marketplace.

Other research designs were not adequate for this study. A quasi-experimental or true experimental design, for example, involves the control of some or all of the variables (Neuman, 2006; Salkind, 2003); however, the variables of cultural intelligence and market orientation could not be controlled because they were distinct to each participant and their organizational environment. Quasi and true experimental designs require the researcher to manipulate the study conditions of some participants for a comparison to those participants in non-manipulated conditions (Neuman, 2006). Exploratory and descriptive designs also did not fit the study parameters, since both designs help clarify the roles of the variables; however, the study variables were well understood to have positive effects on firms globalizing and penetrating the global market.

The correlational research design enabled a variety of statistical analyses of the collected quantitative data. Descriptive statistical analysis and the calculation of Spearman's rho (ρ) coefficient provided calculable evidence of any relationship that may exist between the variables. Correlation analysis provided evidence if significant linear relationships existed between cultural intelligence and market orientation (Triola, 2005). The Spearman's rho (ρ) coefficient and resulting correlational matrix disclosed the correlation's strength, direction, and degree of association (Chen & Popovich, 2002; Cooper & Schindler, 2003).

Theoretical Framework

The theories of cultural intelligence and market orientation were linked in this research as the theoretical framework for global market entrance. This framework comprised an interconnection of cultural intelligence and individual-level market orientation on the global scale and sub-factor levels using the Earley and Ang (2003) cultural intelligence model and the Schlosser (2004) individual market orientation model. Both models were validated through formal validation procedures and extensive research, but an extensive literature search provided no results reflecting any link between both theories in the context of successful global engineering market entrance.

Cultural Intelligence Model

The concept of cultural competency has transformed from its early introduction in the late 1970s and continues to be reinvented to reach global and more dynamic audiences. According to Van Dyne, Ang, and Koh (2009), the earlier frameworks used to distinguish and explain cultural competency among nondescript industry decision makers in a growing global marketplace included the prominent Hofstede's Dimensions of Culture framework. This framework focused primarily on cultural knowledge, such as knowing differences in work habits, cultural behaviors, and cultural norms (Hofstede & Hofstede, 2005; Van Dyne, Ang, & Livermore, 2010).

Cultural intelligence contextualized Hofstede's cultural knowledge-based framework with the frameworks of multiple intelligences (Van Dyne, Ang, & Koh, 2009). Gardener's (1993) multiple facets of intelligence and Sternberg and Detterman's (1986) multiple intelligences frameworks, which were germinal sources for Hofstede's framework, led the way to understanding how cultural competency is connected to multiple intelligence studies. Hofstede's configuration of cultural element knowledge reimaged cultural competency to a personal and leadership-based skillset that is congruent to but different from individual emotional intelligence (Livermore, 2010; Sternberg & Detterman, 1986). Earley and Ang's (2003) concept of cultural intelligence was this reimaged framework.

Cultural intelligence, known also as an individual's cultural quotient, focused cultural competency into four individual cultural factors, namely the cognitive, metacognitive, behavioral, and motivational dimensions (Earley & Ang, 2003; Livermore, 2010; Van Dyne, Ang, & Koh, 2009). Part of the conceptual framework for this research was based on this four-component cultural intelligence model. In the context of global market entrance, cultural intelligence, the independent variable in this study, had correlation to an individual's market orientation competencies.

Market Orientation Studies

Market orientation is beneficial and important to firms with regard to market competitiveness and fiscal performance (Schlosser & McNaughton, 2009). Firms use market orientation to delineate better solutions expressly to meet the needs of the market and customers. Narver and Slater (1990) developed the MKTOR scale to measure market orientation based on three behavioral components: customer orientation, competitor orientation, and interfunctional coordination. Jaworski and Kohli (1993) followed with a different interpretation of market orientation and suggested that market orientation is built upon three components: intelligence generation, intelligence dissemination, and responsiveness. This three-component model is a firm-level construct and is used to measure organizational market orientation through the MARKOR scale (Jaworski & Kohli, 1993).

Various firm-level models and instruments have been developed based upon the Jaworski and Kohli (1993) and Narver and Slater (1990) models; however, these alternate models were specifically designed to meet the needs of distinct markets and businesses. Deng and Dart's (1994) model, for example, incorporated business prosperity on the MKTOR model; Lado, Olivares, and Rivera's model focused on stakeholders; and Farrell and Oczkowski's (1998) model attempted to bridge MKTOR and MARKOR (Tomášková, 2009). As another variant of these germinal works, this current research involved the individual-level variation of the MARKOR scale called the I-MARKOR, which transfigures the three firm-level components to an individual level construct (Schlosser, 2004; Schlosser & McNaughton, 2009). The I-MARKOR focuses on the information acquisition, information sharing, and strategic response capacity of individual decision makers (Schlosser & McNaughton, 2009).

The theoretical framework for this research comprised a connection among the four components of cultural intelligence with the three components of individual market orientation in the context of U.S. engineering firms entering the global market. Both cultural intelligence and market orientation are well-studied concepts and play an integral part in business profitability (Narver & Slater, 1999; Scholl, 2009; Vytlacil, 2010). The research encompassed an attempt to find any relationships between both theoretical constructs in relation to U.S.-based engineering decision makers and the successful entrance into the global marketplace.

Model Relationships to be Tested

The research map in Figure 1 depicts the relationships that were tested and analyzed in the study as related with the theoretical framework. Testing cultural intelligence and individual-level market orientation, including the components that make up each, provided relational information useful in global marketplace decision making. This research map highlights the study with regard to the research question and hypotheses.

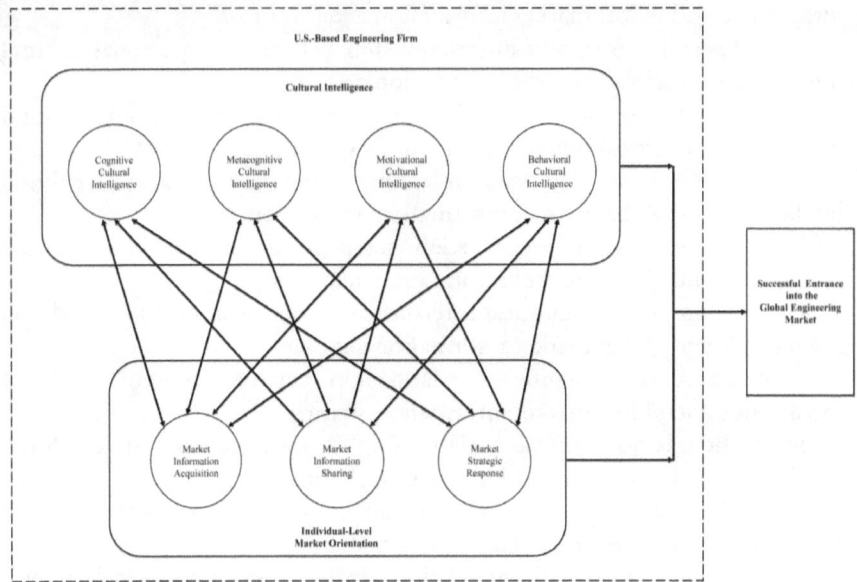

Figure 1. Research map of individual-level relationships.

Research Question and Hypotheses

According to Johnson and Christenson (2012), research questions are developed to address the study's purpose statement as one or more questions that the researcher wants to answer. Research questions are critical to any research project and are an essential component of the researcher's planning and data collection processes. In addressing the study's purpose, the following research question was studied: What relationship exists between the cultural intelligence and global market orientation of decision makers at U.S.-based engineering organizations entering the global marketplace?

For quantitative studies, one or more hypotheses are developed by the researcher to complement the study's research question. Hypotheses form a predictive statement to be tested about the relationship between the study's variables (Neuman, 2006). Salkind (2003) stated that "a good hypothesis poses a question in a testable form" (p. 8). Based on the research question, the hypotheses for this study follow:

H_{O1}: There is no significant relationship between cognitive cultural intelligence and global market information acquisition.

H_{A1}: There is a significant relationship between cognitive cultural intelligence and global market information acquisition.

H_{O2}: There is no significant relationship between metacognitive cultural intelligence and global market information acquisition.

H_{A2}: There is a significant relationship between metacognitive cultural intelligence and global market information acquisition.

$H_{Ø3}$: There is no significant relationship between motivational cultural intelligence and global market information acquisition.

H_{A3}: There is a significant relationship between motivational cultural intelligence and global market information acquisition.

$H_{Ø4}$: There is no significant relationship between behavioral cultural intelligence and global market information acquisition.

H_{A4}: There is a significant relationship between behavioral cultural intelligence and global market information acquisition.

$H_{Ø5}$: There is no significant relationship between cognitive cultural intelligence and global market information sharing.

H_{A5}: There is a significant relationship between cognitive cultural intelligence and global market information sharing.

$H_{Ø6}$: There is no significant relationship between metacognitive cultural intelligence and global market information sharing.

H_{A6}: There is a significant relationship between metacognitive cultural intelligence and global market information sharing.

$H_{Ø7}$: There is no significant relationship between motivational cultural intelligence and global market information sharing.

H_{A7}: There is a significant relationship between motivational cultural intelligence and global market information sharing.

$H_{Ø8}$: There is no significant relationship between behavioral cultural intelligence and global market information sharing.

H_{A8}: There is a significant relationship between behavioral cultural intelligence and global market information sharing.

$H_{Ø9}$: There is no significant relationship between cognitive cultural intelligence and global market strategic response.

H_{A9}: There is a significant relationship between cognitive cultural intelligence and global market strategic response.

$H_{Ø10}$: There is no significant relationship between metacognitive cultural intelligence and global market strategic response.

H_{A10}: There is a significant relationship between metacognitive cultural intelligence and global market strategic response.

$H_{Ø11}$: There is no significant relationship between motivational cultural intelligence and global market strategic response.

H_{A11}: There is a significant relationship between motivational cultural intelligence and global market strategic response.

$H_{Ø12}$: There is no significant relationship between behavioral cultural intelligence and global market strategic response.

H_{A12}: There is a significant relationship between behavioral cultural intelligence and global market strategic response.

Definitions

Several key terms are related to U.S. engineering firms entering the non-U.S. market. The following definitions are intended to provide a unified understanding for the study. Note that certain terms, such as *globalization* and *culture*, hold common variant definitions and warrant further term clarification.

Business custom. A manner of business conduct or practice laced in tradition or societal use inherent in a specific industry, country, location, or community. Business customs include greeting behaviors, business protocols, and cultural understandings (Chaney & Martin, 2006).

Country-of-origin. The term country-of-origin implies the country of origination for products or services. In global marketing and business, the term also relates to a consumer effect characterized by "the tendency among individuals to infer the quality of a product from its country of manufacture" (Ferguson, Dadzie, & Johnston, 2008, p. 429).

Cultural intelligence, also referred to as *Cultural Quotient (CQ)*. Cultural Intelligence is a personal aptitude to work, interact, and manage in a cross-cultural and diverse environment (Ang et al., 2007).

Cross-cultural competence, also referred to as *multicultural competence* or *intercultural competence*. Cross-cultural competence is the ability to operate effectively in a different culture (Gertsen, 1990) and "understand and constructively relate to the uniqueness of each client in light of the diverse cultures that influence each person's perspectives" (Stuart, 2004, p. 6).

Culture. According to Hofstede and Hofstede (2005), culture is "the collective programming of the mind that distinguishes the members of one group or category of people from another" (p. 400). In this study, the term *culture* was enhanced to include ethnicity, nationalism, business, and societal values, customs, and beliefs.

Globalization. Stonehouse, Campbell, Hamill, and Purdie (2004) stated that "globalization refers to the development of global or worldwide business activities, competition and markets and the increasing global interdependence of national economies" (p. 5).

Global mindset. Global mindset refers to "the incorporation of national culture, cross-cultural considerations, international policy and regulatory compliance" in the marketplace (Vieth & Smith, 2008, p. 49).

Glocal. This portmanteau blends the words *global* and *local* to represent the leadership standpoint of thinking globally, but acting locally (Cobley, 2004).

Marketing. The American Marketing Association defines marketing as "the activity, set of institutions, and processes for creating, communicating, delivering, and exchanging offerings that have value for customers, clients, partners, and society at large" (American Marketing Association, 2007, para. 2).

Market orientation. Market orientation is a marketing concept that involves the development of market information regarding client needs, information sharing within the organization, and the resulting organizational response (Kohli, Jaworski, & Kumar, 1993). Schlosser (2004) advanced this idea, defining individual market orientation as a mix of information acquisition, information sharing, and strategic responsive.

Multinational Corporation. Companies that have "separate businesses in separate countries under common ownership" (Drucker, 1997, p. 3).

Scope and Assumptions

This quantitative research was designed to analyze the relationship between the individual cultural intelligence and market orientation of decision makers at domestic engineering organizations entering the global market. This research was based on four assumptions. The first assumption was that a globally-focused engineering service firm is multi-disciplined, including such disciplines as electrical, civil, structural, mechanical, industrial, geotechnical, and chemical engineering. McGraw-Hill Companies (2009) does not delineate global and international engineering design firms by any specific engineering discipline.

The second assumption was that participants were honest and open in their survey responses. Candid answers to survey questions can provide substantive information about the subject and when applied in the context of an organization can help identify best practices and practices that are faltering, ineffective, and ripe for improvement (Church & Waclawski, 1998). The third assumption was that participants have the adequate linguistic and writing ability to convey their perceptions and lived experiences accurately and within the proper context of the study.

The fourth and final assumption was that the global engineering marketplace is a desirable and potentially lucrative marketplace. Acosta et al. (2010) stated how engineering firms have moved onto a worldwide stage where once domestic-only firms now compete globally to stay economically balanced and survive. Building business globally helps flatten the global competitive field and develops a robust and advantageous service delivery network (Fung, Fung, & Wind, 2008).

Limitations and Delimitations
Study Limitations

The research had potential limitations stemming from the study's participation and generalizability of the findings to the population. The generalizability of the results was a potential limiter to the study. The participants in the research were executive decision makers from the top U.S.-based globalized engineering firms. With a population from American engineering companies, study results might not be generalizable to decision makers from non-American engineering firms. Different approaches toward the points on the Likert-type scale, including interpretation, response style, and use of the scale, served as another limitation for participation in the study (Church & Waclawski, 1998; Neuman, 2006). Because the study involved a differing number of participants from each organization due to participant availability, random selection, and choice, the differing level of organizational participation posed a potential risk of sample bias. Likewise, the exclusion of potential data from non-participating decision makers posed a possible threat to the statistical validity of the findings.

Study Delimitations

The study was focused on firms with a U.S. country-of-origin (Lin & Kao, 2004). The U.S.-based engineering firms used in the study were identified as top international or global engineering firms by ENR magazine. The study focused only on the cultural intelligence factors of cognitive, metacognitive, behavioral, and motivational elements, as measured with the multidimensional Cultural Intelligence Scale (CQS), and the market orientation factors of information acquisition, information sharing, and strategic response, as measured by the Schlosser (2004) I-MARKOR market orientation instrument. This study did not involve measurement of organizational cultural intelligence competence, organizational market orientation competence, or the competencies of one population over another. The study was not designed to measure cultural intelligence and market orientation competencies, or lack thereof, from single-discipline, temperately successful, or embryonic global engineering firms. The constraints in population size and population composition, which was characterized by successful global engineering work, limited the findings from the research. The study was designed to survey participants who had access to the Internet.

Rationale and Significance of the Study

Little research has been conducted specific to globally focused engineering firms regarding cross-cultural competencies (Acosta et al., 2010). Conversely, market orientation has been deeply studied. The relationship between market orientation and organization-wide cross-cultural competencies has not been rigorously evaluated. Determining if a relationship exists yielded information that might help leaders and decision makers develop successful strategies for global marketplace entry. The study contained engineering industry, organizational leadership, and global marketing significance. The results contributed to the body of knowledge particularly regarding individual cross-cultural behaviors, cognition, meta-cognition, and motivations in relation to global market information acquisition, information sharing, and strategic responsive. The results indicated relationships between global decision makers' cultural intelligence and market orientation that leaders from other organizations can apply in their own global business strategies. These revisited global strategies potentially may enhance their chances for success in the competitive global market. The results can help leaders understand how cross-cultural competency, namely the four components of cultural intelligence, related with the three primary factors of market orientation. This relational knowledge might support global engineering leadership approaches to non-U.S. market campaigns and penetrations.

Current global engineering strategies relating to cultural differentiation are varied and are inclined to exist in organizations as proprietary information. This study can supply engineering leaders who have little to no global market success with an understanding of how cross-cultural knowledge and strategic orientation to the specific market can benefit their global campaigns for new work and help them to grow as intercultural leaders. According to Prahalad (1997), intercultural competence has become an important discriminator for firms and a point of impetus for leaders to acknowledge different values and beliefs. Engineering firms facing sustainability and survival issues from the increased domestic competition and decision makers desiring new markets to penetrate might benefit from the focus on cross-cultural and market orientation competencies.

For many leaders, cultural intelligence is not intuitive (Livermore, 2010; Ng, Tan, & Ang, 2011). The significance of cultural intelligence derived from the participant responses might indicate transferable cross-cultural leadership traits that can enhance the efficacy of global campaigns on both the marketing and work capture fronts. This study delineated the importance or lack of importance for each cultural intelligence and market orientation factor. Ultimately, the study findings derived from participant responses may be a credible source of useful global business intelligence for interested domestic engineering firms.

Chapter Summary and Organization of the Study

Faced with increasing domestic competition from non-U.S. firms and a growing global marketplace, U.S.-based engineering firms have turned their focus to globalizing their services. Understanding the multifaceted cultural aspects of marketing and penetrating the global engineering market requires heightened cross-cultural leadership competencies in tandem with a strategic market orienting activities. Cultural intelligence is a burgeoning concept designed to distinguish an individual's ability to adapt to unfamiliar cultural environments. Cultural intelligence blends four distinct components of an individual's cultural understanding, namely cognitive, metacognitive, behavioral, and motivational elements (Earley & Ang, 2003; Livermore, 2010; Mannor, 2008). Market orientation is a concept that involves the development of market information regarding client needs and customs, the sharing of information, and the organization's response (Kohli, Jaworski, & Kumar, 1993). Schlosser (2004) applied market orientation to the individuals making decisions, and outlined three components of individual market orientation as information acquisition, information sharing, and market strategic response.

The purpose of the quantitative, correlational research study was to understand the relationships between the independent variables, cultural intelligence and market orientation, within U.S.-based engineering firms aimed at the dependent variable, entrance in the global marketplace. Since there was a significant relationship between cultural intelligence and individual market orientation, global-looking domestic engineering firms are encouraged to invest deeper in enhancing the factors that comprise cultural intelligent leadership decisions in the organization. The study was bounded by the question: What relationship exists between the cultural intelligence and global market orientation of decision makers at U.S.-based engineering organizations entering the global marketplace?

Possible relationships in this research study were identified through the use of an online questionnaire with two parts. The first part involved a survey based on the Ang et al.'s (2007) Cultural Intelligence Scale to measure the individual's cognitive, meta-cognitive, behavioral, and motivational cultural intelligence factors. The second part involved the Schlosser (2004) I-MARKOR market orientation scale, which measures an individual's ability to gather, disseminate, and respond to market intelligence. The population of the research study was composed of senior-level global engineering and marketing decision makers based in the U.S. Chapter 2 presents germinal, historic, and current literature in the areas of global engineering organizations, cultural intelligence, market orientation, and organizational performance.

TWO

LITERATURE REVIEW

The research topic was introduced in chapter 1 along with the problem, purpose, significance, and background of the study. The purpose of this quantitative correlational study was to determine any relationship that may exist between the independent variables of cultural intelligence and market orientation of decision makers at U.S.-based engineering firms to the dependent variable of entering the global marketplace. To measure the relationships, the study involved the use of a survey joining the Multidimensional Cultural Intelligence Scale (CQS) scale for measuring cultural intelligence and the individual MARKOR (I-MARKOR) scale to measure individual market orientation.

Chapter 2 presents a thorough discussion of the germinal and current literature on cultural intelligence and market orientation. The discussion permits a strong understanding of this study's variables and brings into context the effects of the variables (cultural intelligence and market orientation) on organizational performance and marketplace success. This chapter begins with a brief discussion of the literature review process, which includes conducting searches on peer-reviewed titles, articles, research documents, journals, and other literature and media. Past and current literature within the last five years (2008-2013) that has explored or investigated the relationship of cultural intelligence with market orientation in a global engineering context is scant. Following the brief discussion on literature review process is the study's literature review.

Chapter 2 presents a literature review containing three main sections: national culture, cultural intelligence, and market orientation. The first section, national culture, provides insight into how cultural intelligence arose from the recognition that cultures are different globally. The second section, cultural intelligence, includes traditional views on psychometric models of intelligence, multiple intelligence theory, the culture-intelligence relationship, and predominant cultural intelligence models. The section covers Earley and Ang's (2003) four-factor model, which is used in this study, and provides further detail into the factors of the model. The section concludes with research related to Ang et al.'s (2007) Cultural Intelligence Scale and information about the influence cultural intelligence has on organizational performance.

The third section, market orientation, contains the germinal research that has served as the foundation for current market orientation perspectives, including the multitude of market orientation definitions and traditional approaches to market orientation measurement. The section progresses from the firm-level models of market orientation to Schlosser's (2004) individual-level model used in this study. Schlosser and McNaughton's (2009) I-MARKOR scale is discussed in detail and research is presented on the cultural aspects of market orientation, global market orientation, and the relationship to organizational performance. The chapter concludes with discussion on the need for leaders and decision makers at U.S.-based engineering firms to identify and use cultural intelligence with a global-facing market orientation to better prepare for the global engineering marketplace.

Title Searches, Articles, Research Documents, and Journals

The intent of this study was to determine the relationship between cultural intelligence and market orientation in U.S.-based engineering firms entering the global marketplace. The research was drawn from the concepts of cultural intelligence (Earley & Ang, 2003), market orientation (Kohli & Jaworski, 1990; Jaworski & Kohli, 1993), and individual market orientation (Schlosser, 2004). The research was applied to the contexts of U.S. country-of-origin engineering firms and the global engineering market.

Title searches were performed to find existing literature about cultural intelligence, culture, cross-cultural competency, market orientation, client orientation, marketing orientation, globalization, and global engineering. Since cultural intelligence and market orientation are multi-faceted concepts, key search terms were limited to the focus of individual-level market orientation and cultural intelligence. Primary search locations and databases included EBSCOhost Database, ProQuest Database, Gale PowerSearch, IBISWorld, Plunkett Research Online, Sage Journals Online, Journal of Marketing Research, Journal of International Marketing, the Cultural Intelligence Center, and the World Wide Web. There were no access limitations to any of the research sites, either online or through public and university library systems.

Table 1 categorizes the number of materials used for this research effort, particularly with regard to the main topics and instruments related to the research. The table details the research sources, including peer-reviewed articles, books and book chapters, websites, and other research materials.

In using the World Wide Web, the terms cross-cultural competency, culture, and global engineering were too expansive and required further narrowing and definition to obtain useful results. The other terms, such as market orientation, cultural intelligence, and globalization, provided targeted and relevant results. These useful results generally involved highlights of existing and relevant studies that similarly were found in the other research database results, obscured in other database search results, or missing from database search results. Ultimately, research conducted on the World Wide Web served as the impetus for database searches for specific journal articles.

Table 1

Quantification of literature sources used for this research effort, including peer-reviewed articles, books and book chapters, websites, and other research materials

Topic	Peer-reviewed article	Book/ Chapter	Website/ blog	Other[a]
Correlational studies	3	6	1	1
Cultural context of market orientation	12	2	0	1
Cultural intelligence	21	19	0	4
CQS	8	6	1	2
Cultural models	19	13	3	4
Global engineering	9	4	2	5
Globalization / global marketing	17	11	1	3
I-MARKOR scale	3	0	0	1
Individual market orientation	2	1	0	5
Global market orientation	4	1	1	0
Market orientation	36	8	2	3
Multiple intelligences	1	6	2	1
Organizational performance	12	6	0	4
Psychometric models of intelligence	4	4	2	0
Total / percentage	151	87	15	34
	52.61%	30.31%	5.23%	11.85%

Note. [a] Other category includes conference papers, technical reports, white papers, unpublished research reports and papers, dissertations, theses, manuals, and statistical databases.

National Culture

The concept of cultural intelligence arose from research conducted to identify, understand, classify, and quantify national culture (Early & Ang, 2003; Livermore, 2006). Earley and Ang (2003) distinguished the importance of national culture through dominance in cultural research, but recognized that a values-based cultural model had research limitations that forced further research to be done. A significant research limitation involved the inability to discriminate individual-level cultural understanding. Elenkov and Pimentel (2008) specified that the various national culture dimensions reflect country level cultural trends and allowed for the emergence of cultural intelligence and the examination of the individual-level construct. Thomas and Inkson (2009) added that the national culture values research revealed the existence of differences between individualism and collectivism among cultural perspectives.

The characteristics of national culture as defined through this antecedent research offer a useful and important context to the concept of cultural intelligence (Rogers, 2008). Livermore (2009) suggested one vital contribution of national culture research is in the application of cultural intelligence by individuals within and across national cultures. Adding credence for examination in this study, Venaik and Brewer (2010) added that for international business research these national culture models are among the most prevalent cross-cultural dimensional models used today. The following subsections detail the significant antecedent national culture research, particularly Hofstede's five national culture dimensions, the GLOBE study, Trompenaar's dimensions of cultural differences, and the two iterations of Schwartz's value dimensions. Examining these national cultural models will provide insight into the development and implications of cultural intelligence.

Hofstede's Five Dimensions to National Culture

As indicated from the different models relating intelligence with culture, recognizing different cultures is important for the understanding of general intelligence, the measurement of that intelligence, and the cultural thought processes and decisions made (Sternberg, 2007). Hofstede brought the idea of intelligence as related to national culture into the worldwide view. According to Venaik and Brewer (2010), Hofstede's additions to the culture knowledgebase involved the development of characteristics (called dimensions) that, when measured for a population, provides an average value for national culture attributes.

Hofstede's (1980) cultural dimension model was founded upon his research in the 1970s of International Business Machines (known as IBM), a large multinational technology company. Hofstede surveyed over 100,000 IBM employees across 50 countries primarily for individualism and collectivism traits and gave countries a score. Hofstede and Hofstede (2005), built upon his earlier findings and initial model (Hofstede, 1980), detailed five dimensions to national culture that help discriminate the differences in basic cultural values. These dimensions to national culture are power distance, individualism/collectivism, masculinity/femininity, uncertainty avoidance, and long and short-term orientation (de Mooij, 2010; Hofstede & Hofstede, 2005).

According to Sivakumar and Nakata (2001), the *power distance* dimension indicates the degree to which differences in prosperity, affluence, and other benefactions are accepted within a culture. The power distance dimension elucidates social inequalities in a culture and characterizes the "relationship with authority" (Minkov & Hofstede, 2011, p. 12). Hofstede's *individualism/collectivism* dimension indicates the degree of individuality, societal and familial ties, and in-group fidelity in a culture (de Mooij, 2010; Hofstede & Hofstede, 2005; Sivakumar & Nakata, 2001). The *masculinity/femininity* dimension marks the degree of defined masculine values, which include achievement and aggression, with defined feminine values, which include caring for others and quality of life (de Mooij, 2010; Sivakumar & Nakata, 2001).

Hofstede's *uncertainty avoidance* dimension indicates the degree to which cultures evade ambiguous situations through the organization of predictable and recognizable situations (de Mooij, 2010; Venaik & Brewer, 2010). The avoidance of uncertainty is a common theme in cross-cultural studies as detailed by Hofstede and Hofstede (2005) and the Global Leadership and Organizational Behavior Effectiveness (GLOBE) cultural project (House, Hanges, Javidan, Dorfman, & Gupta, 2004) and surfaces in organizational cultures. As with national cultures, organizational cultures generally aim to avoid uncertain situations for the sake of company sustainability. Notably, Weick and Sutcliffe (2007) suggested that the awareness of environmental impacts should be a process integrated into an organization's culture to avoid the unexpected. Heightened awareness can help avoid unwelcome situations and serve as a predictive measure. This process leads to better predictions of what is going to occur, which, ultimately, leads to a mindful and resilient strategic organization (Weick & Sutcliffe, 2007). This cultural dimension is perhaps far more reaching than what was originally intended, which is why Hofstede's dimensions collectively have an important role in global marketing campaigns and, correspondingly, global market orientation.

Lastly, Hofstede's *long-term/short-term orientation* dimension was an addition to Hofstede's original model and was a concept born from discussions of past, present, and future events with the uncertainty avoidance dimension (Minkov & Hofstede, 2011). Long-term orientation represents the nurturing of cultural qualities that are oriented toward future gains and beneficial outcomes, while short-term orientation represents the nurturing of cultural qualities that are oriented toward the past and present (Hofstede & Hofstede, 2005). Similar to the uncertainty avoidance dimension, the long-term/short-term orientation dimension holds significance with national cultures and organizational cultures alike. This dimension has direct correlations to cultural intelligence, whereby individuals who are culturally intelligent acknowledge the current characteristics, expectations, and future trends of different cultures (Mannor, 2008). As indicated earlier, Hofstede's cultural dimensions served as a predecessor to the GLOBE study, which has also served as foundational research for the development of the cultural intelligence model.

The GLOBE Study

The Global Leadership and Organizational Behavior Effectiveness study, more commonly known as the GLOBE Study, was conducted in the mid-1990s to determine similarities and differences in cultural values across different countries. Researchers for the GLOBE study grouped sixty-two countries into ten distinct clusters based upon similar cultural attributes. The goal of the GLOBE study was to develop cross-cultural information about major nations throughout the world for individuals who needed to interact internationally (Shi & Wang, 2011; Thomas & Inkson, 2009).

The GLOBE study's clusters were based upon the following nine cultural dimensions: Uncertainty Avoidance, Power Distance, Institutional Collectivism, In-Group Collectivism, Gender Egalitarianism, Assertiveness, Future Orientation, Performance Orientation, and Humane Orientation (House et al., 2004). Similar to Hofstede's model, the GLOBE study's *uncertainty avoidance* dimension takes consideration to the prevention and circumvention of unknown situations through the reliance of societal norms, while the similar *power distance* dimension regards the degree of acceptance of unequal cultural power sources. According to Venaik and Brewer (2010), although both studies hold similar cultural values for each dimension, the GLOBE study has contradictions with the Hofstede study regarding the practices involved with uncertainty avoidance. This summarily means that both studies have found comparable results for the cultural appreciation for uncertainty avoidance, but dissimilar results for the cultural practices related to avoiding uncertainty. Venaik and Brewer (2010) concluded that this discrepancy between the studies has generated a need for further study and cultural analysis.

GLOBE's *institutional collectivism* dimension indicates the degree to which resource distribution is rewarded through organizational or societal practices. The study's *in-group collectivism* dimension indicates the degree to which individuals show loyalty and cohesiveness within an organization or within a society (Magnusson, Wilson, Zdravkovic, Zhou, & Westjohn, 2008; Thomas & Inkson, 2009). This dimension showcases the linkage between national cultures and the organizations and individuals within these cultures, and particularly serves as an important research toward individual cultural intelligence. In fact, Thomas and Inkson (2009) stated that with "the GLOBE cultural clusters, you can get a first approximation of the extent to which you might share cultural values with people from other societies" (p. 39).

The *assertiveness* dimension, perhaps the last individual-focused characteristic of the study, indicates the degree individuals are assertive with other individuals in different cultures and societies (Magnusson et al., 2008; Thomas & Inkson, 2009). The nature of this dimension has distinct correlations to behaviors of cultural intelligent individuals. The remaining GLOBE study dimensions, namely *gender egalitarianism, future orientation, performance orientation, humane orientation* are particular to cultures as a whole and appear to have little direct correlation or impact on individual cultural intelligence. Hofstede and the GLOBE studies laid important foundations for national data of cultural values within cross-cultural research and created pathways for further studies such as Trompenaars' dimensions of cultural differences.

Trompenaars' Dimensions of Cultural Differences

Taking a slightly different approach to national culture than Hofstede, Trompenaars developed a model of differences in national cultures that was developed using questions about everyday life dilemmas. According to Magnusson et al. (2008) and Trompenaars and Hampden-Turner (1998), Trompenaars' dimensions of cultural differences were founded upon Parson's (1951) sociological dimensions with two added dimensions to satisfy cultural attitudes toward time and the environment. Trompenaars' model consists of seven cultural dimensions that clarify various interactions between individuals from different cultures. These dimensions have direct implications to individuals having leadership and decision making tasks in different cultures. Explicitly, Mannor (2008) and de Mooij (2010) independently posited that Trompenaars' dimensions of cultural difference can support the understanding of how culturally-different leaders approach and resolve organizational problems.

The first dimension, *universalism versus particularism*, identifies a culture's focus and following of either defined rulings or specific relationships. The second dimension, *individualism versus communitarianism* (also identified as *collectivism*), relates to the regard of oneself as either an individual or part of a group. This dimension has relevance to both cultural intelligence and market orientation, whereby both understandings can be measured on individual and organizational levels. The third dimension, *neutral versus emotional*, identifies differences between cultural interactions as either objective or emotional actions. The fourth dimension, *specific versus diffuse*, relates to the type of business interaction in a culture, either through a personal contact and relationship or through specific contract or contract prescription. The fifth dimension, *achievement versus ascription*, defines how individuals are acknowledged: by proof of accomplishment or by a prescribed stature or connections. The sixth dimension, *attitudes to time*, which delineates how cultures value past and current achievements and experience. This dimension also depicts cultural expectations regarding doing tasks sequentially one at a time or by multi-tasking. The seventh dimension, *attitudes to the environment*, relates cultural differences in belief as to whether individuals control their environment or the environment controls the individual (Trompenaars & Hampden-Turner, 1998).

Smith, Dugan, and Trompenaars (1996) analyzed the initial five dimensions of cultural differences among 43 nations around the words and found some relationships with Hofstede's cultural dimensions and Schwartz's value dimensions, which are discussed later. A major weakness in the multi-nation study is that no national scores for Trompenaars' dimensions were produced in the findings. According to de Mooij (2010), the lack of national scores renders this multi-national study useless for marketing. Trompenaars' dimensions have limited relevance to cultural intelligence concepts, which is illustrated by the lack of citation and reference in most of the germinal and current cultural intelligence research. Earley and Ang (2003) stated that Trompenaars' approach and other values-based approaches to culture have limited value to cultural intelligence research, primarily due to the impersonal and rigid cultural value system as well as the lack of a cognitive approach. They continued with their belief that new approaches toward culture perhaps would provide more auspicious results.

Schwartz's Collective Value Dimensions

Perhaps one of the more fitting cultural studies with regard to cultural intelligence was Schwartz's value survey for dimensions of national culture. Like the studies previously described, Schwartz's (1994) cultural values study is also based on the assumption that within a single country there is cultural homogeneity. According to Thomas and Inkson (2009), Schwartz based his value dimensions model on a belief that every culture subscribes to three common requirements: 1) a need to distinguish how individuals respond outside their society; 2) a need for societal sustainability; and 3) a need to distinguish how society response to the natural world. Schwartz's first universal requirement has applicability to cultural intelligence given the individual nature of the cultural response.

Surveying 41 cultural groups across 38 countries with a desire to compare different cultures, Schwartz (1994, 1999) developed seven value dimensions, which were:

1) *Conservatism*: Upholding a cultural status quo where individuals are part of a collective group.

2) *Affective autonomy*: The individual pursuit of distinctly positive experiences.

3) *Intellectual autonomy*: The individual pursuit of one's own concepts and intellectual pathways.

4) *Hierarchy*: Similar to the power distance dimensions from other studies, the hierarchy value dimension identifies the unequal nature of power distribution within a culture.

5) *Egalitarianism:* The cultural recognition that individuals from other cultures are equals and of equal morals.

6) *Mastery*: The cultural exploitation of outside environments, including the social environment and the natural world.

7) *Harmony*: The cultural competence of fitting into outside environments harmoniously, contrary to any exploitation of outside environments.

Schwartz (1994, 1999) had a similar ideology to Hofstede (1980), Trompenaars (1994), and Globe (House et al., 2004) regarding the notion that within each culture there are homogeneous values and norms. Principally, individuals within a culture are guided by that culture's perspectives. Where these cultural studies differ is with the particular cultural values they measure. Schwartz's study, well beyond the other studies, holds strong links to individual cultural intelligence. Since Schwartz's survey results were based on responses based on individual experience, his value dimensions can be analyzed on an individual level as well as the country level (Schwartz, 1994).

Schwartz's Individual Value Dimensions

Schwartz and Bardi (2001) further explored Schwartz's value dimensions on the individual level examining individual value differences and defining ten individual level value types. The authors found that "individuals both within and across societies have quite different value priorities that reflect their different genetic heritage, personal experiences, social locations, and enculturation" (p. 268). The individual level of analysis allowed deeper examination of the cultural value dimensions as they related to the development and independent decisions within different cultures. Ng, Lee, and Soutar (2007) stated that examination at an individual level exposes what particular values are important to individuals within a culture and what values are viewed as less important.

The individual level values defined by Schwartz and Bardi (2007) are: power, achievement, hedonism, stimulation, self-direction, universalism, benevolence, tradition, conformity, and security. *Power* refers to social status and individual presence and influence among others. *Achievement* refers to individual success and competency. *Hedonism* refers individual enjoyment, pleasure, and positivity. *Stimulation* denotes an individual's enthusiasm and personal challenges. *Self-Direction* refers to independent thinking and decision making. *Universalism* represents individual acknowledgement of other individuals and outside environments. *Benevolence* refers to individual acknowledgement and pursuance of the wellbeing of others who are generally within your contact. *Tradition* denotes an individual respect for culture and religious differences. *Conformity* refers to an individual's control of personal actions and engagements that may infringe cultural expectations. Lastly, *Security* denotes an individual's holistic approach to personal and cultural safety and stability.

Schwartz and Bardi (2007) concluded that the individual-level value dimensions revealed deep distinctions between group cultures and across societal cultures, and that these distinctions are directly related to individual behaviors. Thomas and Inkson (2003) suggested that Schwartz's (1994) work on value dimensions laid a foundational understanding of the relationship between an individual and the group, the natural world, and the preservation of society. Both Schwartz's (1994) and Schwartz and Bardi's (2001) studies presented important research groundwork for cultural intelligence. An individual's understanding of their culture facilitates comparisons to other cultures, and ultimately serves as a necessary stepping-stone to becoming culturally intelligent (Thomas & Inkson, 2003).

Cultural Intelligence

This section begins with a discussion about predecessor research on general intelligence, multiple intelligences, the relationship of intelligence to culture, and the lead in to the concept of cultural intelligence. Earley and Ang's (2003) initial model of cultural intelligence is discussed with highlights of the various other major cultural intelligence models. This section continues with coverage of the four-factor model used in this study and the quantitative scale for measuring cultural intelligence, appropriately named the Cultural Intelligence Scale (CQS). This section concludes with a discussion about the relationship between cultural intelligence and organizational performance.

Defining and Measuring Intelligence

Cultural intelligence theory has emerged from the numerous theories developed to understand human intelligence better. Psychometrics, the first formal scientific approach to define and measure intelligence, began gaining popularity in the early 20th Century. In 1905, Binet and Simon created a scale that measured mental abilities related to academics, such as knowledge, comprehension, memory, numerical reasoning, time awareness and idea combination. In 1908 and 1911, the Binet-Simon scale was revised and enhanced to better measure the general mental capabilities or intelligence (Earley & Ang, 2003; Multiple Intelligences Institute, 2008).

In 1912, Stern developed the initial concept of an intelligence quotient, or IQ, which is the ratio between mental age and chronological age. The concept of Intelligence Quotient gained popularity in 1916 through Terman, a psychometrician who revised Stern's IQ concept as the Stanford-Binet Intelligence Scale and developed a paper-based version. This paper-based version was used to administer the intelligence test on individuals and became a staple in academics. IQ tests are still used today (Earley & Ang, 2003; Multiple Intelligences Institute, 2008)

Psychometric tests of intelligence, like Stern and Terman's intelligence scales, were focused at determining the core mental aptitude or a general factor (referred to as g) of individual intelligence. From these initial concepts of intelligence rose other psychometric models that took a structural approach to intelligence with a sharp focus on individual mental ability. Most notably was Spearman's theory of general human ability (Earley & Ang, 2003).

Through his psychometric theory of human intelligence, Spearman's (1927) presented a two-factor theory of intelligence that comprised of a general factor g and one or more specific factors s. Spearman's g represents "a fixed amount of 'mental energy' that an individual assigns to a specific task" (Earley & Ang, 2003, p. 40). His s factor can comprise one or more factors (s_1, s_2, s_3...s_n) that are unique to the task at hand. According to Sternberg (2007), Spearman's g general factor is a broadly established theory of intelligence and served as an antecedent to later academic and non-academic theories of intelligence.

Spearman's theory was foundational but subject to criticism from such psychometric theorists as Thomson, Thurstone, Guilford, Vernon and Carroll. Thompson agreed with Spearman on the idea of a general factor for mental ability, but believed the general factor had multiple sources of differentiation among individuals. Thurstone, too, accepted Spearman's g factor, but remained dubious of the inherent value of the general factor and suggested Spearman's general factor was of subordinate importance. Thurstone posited that intelligence was multi-faceted and consisted of seven distinct factors of mental ability: verbal comprehension, word fluency, number facility, spatial visualization, associative memory, perceptual speed, and inductive reasoning (Earley & Ang, 2003; Multiple Intelligences Institute, 2008; Sternberg et al., 2000).

Guilford disagreed with the preceding psychometric theorists and found absolute minimal value in the g factor. He presented his own multi-dimensional structure-of-intellect model, which comprised 150 primary factors, 85 secondary factors, and 16 tertiary factors of mental ability (Earley & Ang, 2003; Sternberg et al., 2000). Unwittingly hinting at some of the aspects of cultural intelligence (particularly cognition, meta-cognition, and behavior), Guilford's factors were organized along three dimensions:

1. *Operational* dimension including such categories as cognition, memory, evaluation, and divergent/convergent production.

2. *Content* dimension including behavioral, symbolic, semantic, and figural categories.

3. *Product* dimension including such categories as units, systems, and implications (Earley & Ang, 2003).

Vernon (1971) took a different approach to psychometrics by modeling intelligence as comprising multiple layers going top down in importance. Vernon's hierarchical approach positioned general cognitive ability (Spearman's g factor) as the top level of intelligence. The second layer comprises the verbal-education and practical-mechanical-spatial aspects to intelligence. The third layer and still lower in importance relative to intelligence breaks down the level two components into four subfactors: verbal and numerical abilities (under verbal-education) and spatial and manual abilities (under practical-mechanical-spatial). The bottom layer of the hierarchy and lowest in importance is dedicated to specific group factors (Earley & Ang, 2003; Wilson, 2004).

Progressing Vernon's hierarchical theory, Carroll, another psychometrician, proposed his three stratum theory of intelligence. Imagine a pyramid with Stratum I at the base, Stratum II in the middle, and Stratum III at the topmost position. According to Sternberg (2007), Stratum I involves specific mental abilities, such as spelling and speed of reasoning. Stratum II involves broad mental abilities ranging from the ability to view things in an innovative way (known as fluid intelligence) to the effective use of a knowledgebase (Sternberg, 2007; Wilson, 2004). Stratum III involves a single factor of general intelligence similar to Spearman's g (Sternberg, 2007).

These different but progressive psychometric theories of human intelligence ranged in hierarchical and non-hierarchical designs and served as the foundation for development of dynamic multi-factored theories of intelligence (Earley & Ang, 2003). Developed from academic applications, these psychometric theories laid the groundwork for further academic and non-academic intelligence models, including the multiple intelligences theory. Cultural intelligence and other real-world intra-personal (non-academic) intelligences, such as emotional intelligence and social intelligence, are founded on the germinal works related to psychometric models of intelligence (Elenkov & Pimentel, 2008).

Multiple Intelligences. Built on concepts advanced from

psychometric modeling of general intelligence was the acknowledgement that general intelligence is more complex and multi-faceted than just a single coefficient of analysis. This thinking bred the concept of multiple intelligences. Gardner (1983, 2006) detailed his theory of multiple intelligences that initially outlined seven distinct forms of intelligence consisting of:

1. *Musical Intelligence* consists of an individual's aptitude for music particularly with regard to the attention to and presentation, performance, and composition of musical patterns.
2. *Bodily-Kinesthetic Intelligence* involves the whole body approach to problem solving, including mental and physical coordination.
3. *Logical-Mathematical Intelligence* involves an ability of logical problem solving and reasoning, mathematical proficiency, pattern identification, and scientific examination.
4. *Linguistic Intelligence* involves the capability of learning, understanding, and using language to accomplish specific goals. This ability surfaces in both the spoken and written forms of language as well as surfaces in an individual's ability to learn languages and linguistic expression.
5. *Spatial Intelligence* involves distinct awareness of and thinking in relation to physical space, boundaries, and environments.
6. *Interpersonal Intelligence* involves the ability to understand and interact with others, including such traits as empathy, common sense, and real world instincts.
7. *Intrapersonal Intelligence* involves an understanding of one's self, including interests, personal goals, and abilities.

After years of research and peer interaction, Gardner (2006) began questioning whether other forms of intelligences existed. He detailed the potential for naturalistic, spiritual, existential, and moral intelligences, but ultimately decided that there was an eighth distinct form of intelligence: *Naturalistic Intelligence*. According to the Multiple Intelligences Institute (2008), naturalistic intelligence relates to the ability to distinguish among living things, such as animals, flora, fauna, ocean life, and bacteria. Gardner's eighth form of intelligence also involves and an understanding of the natural world features, including landscape and terrain, clouds, and oceans.

Disenfranchised by the historical use of psychometric measurement of human intelligence and discouraged by Gardner's behavioral-focused theory of Multiple Intelligences, Sternberg (1985) developed his Triarchic Theory of Human Intelligence. Earley and Ang (2003) stated that Sternberg's triarchic theory went beyond just the behavioral aspects of intelligence and showcased the internal and external dimensions of intelligence. Sternberg (1985; 2000) stated that his theory was not based on types of intelligences,

like Gardner's theory, but rather his triarchic theory was based on patterns of successful intelligence. After examining intelligence related to gifted individuals, Sternberg (2000) highlighted three distinct components to successful intelligence:
1. The *Analytical* component is a componential dimension to human intelligence that involves the ability to assess and analyze individual ideas and information from others.
2. The *Creative* component is an experiential dimension to human intelligence that involves the ability to develop and apply new approaches and creative solutions to situations or tasks.
3. The *Practical* component is a contextual dimension to human intelligence that involves the ability to adapt to an environment and enact change to transform that environment.

Successful and multiple intelligences theories are relevant to the concept of cultural intelligence. Earley and Ang (2003) stated that Gardner's and Sternberg's theories are the exemplary models that feature perspectives on cognition, behaviors and context related to human intelligence. These authors indicate both theories as precursors to cultural intelligence concepts. Sternberg and Grigorenko (2006) suggested, "successful intelligence is typically defined within a culture" (p. 28). This idea of intelligence defined by culture adds credence that real-world intra-personal (non-academic) intelligences, primarily emotional and social intelligences are other precursors to the cultural intelligence model. To this end, Livermore (2010) stated that cultural intelligence is grounded in multiple intelligences theory.

Intelligence and Culture

Sternberg (2007) explained that there are four dominant models detailing the relationship of culture to intelligence, chronologically named Models I, II, III, and IV. All four models associate similarities and differences between the dimensions of intelligence and the measure of intelligence in the context of multiple cultures. The dimensions of intelligence relate to the analytic, creative, and practical attributes of general intelligence (Sternberg, 2000), while the measurement of intelligence involves how intelligence as a topic is quantified and analyzed. The four models support the comparison and contrast of Sternberg's (2000) triarchic dimensions of intelligence with the measurement of general intelligence within an overarching context of varying cultural environments.

According to Sternberg (2007), Model I, both the dimensions and measurement of intelligence remain the same over different cultures, and support the research of Jensen (1982, 1998) and Eysenck (1986). Jensen (1982, 1998) ascertained that general intelligence is the same cross-culturally throughout varying locations and chronologic times. Eysenck (1986) focused on the physiological mechanics of general intelligence with regard to speed and measurement, and takes the approach that all human general intelligence is the same except for the speed to which information is processed.

Model II portrays that although the dimensions of intelligence are different across cultures, the measurement and testing of intelligence remains the same (Sternberg, 2007). Model II aligns with the research of Nisbett (2003), who contended that using the same measurement methods for intelligence across cultures indicated that individuals in different cultures think differently about problems. Modell III depicts that the dimensions and measurements of intelligence remain constant cross-culturally, but the methods for measurement differ. Sternberg (2007) acknowledged that Model III mimics his own belief regarding the relationship between intelligence and culture.

Lastly, Model IV is a polar opposite of Model I and identifies that both the dimensions and measurements of intelligence are different cross-culturally. This fourth model of intelligence among varying cultures complements the research by Berry (1974) and Sarason and Doris (1979). According to Berry (1974), intelligence can be understood by examining and measuring the factors comprising intelligence within each individual culture. Intelligence within one culture will be different and tested differently than other cultures. Sarason and Doris (1979) take a similar approach toward intelligence and culture and stated that intelligence is a creation of culture and that elements of intelligence common in one culture may not necessarily be common in another. Recognizing these links between intelligence and culture provided adequate foundational understanding for the emergence of Early and Ang's initial cultural intelligence model.

Earley and Ang's Initial Three-Factor Model

According to Earley and Ang (2003), cultural intelligence is: "a person's capability for successful adaptation to new cultural settings, that is, for unfamiliar settings attributable to cultural content" (p. 9). With this premise in mind, Earley and Ang (2003) developed a concrete model for cultural intelligence that comprised of three factors: cognitive, motivational, and behavioral. The authors acknowledged all three factors as pivotal to interacting with different cultures. They also defined the cognitive factor as being dichotic in the sense that cognition has two levels of mental operation: metacognition, which refers to higher thinking about experience and knowledge, and cognition, which refers to the various types of knowledge that form the essence of what we already know (Earley & Ang, 2003). These three factors, including the separation of metacognition are defined later in this chapter under the four factor model discussion. What is importance to recognize is that Earley and Ang's (2003) initial model provided the foundational research for the more advanced and demarcated four factor model used in this study.

Other Cultural Intelligence Models

After the Earley and Ang (2003) model was introduced, the concept of cultural intelligence became an emerging concept within global business circles. Business leaders facing the challenges of globalization and business sustainability quickly realized the importance of understanding different cultures (Livermore, 2010; Thomas & Inkson, 2003). In response, Thomas and Inkson (2003) developed their model for cultural intelligence, complementing the earlier model, and promoted three components to cultural intelligence: knowledge, mindfulness, and behavioral skills. Thomas's (2006) research, which combined the cognitive and metacognitive in a single dimension, served as a predecessor to Thomas and Inkson's (2003, 2009) three-factor model of cultural intelligence. The cultural intelligence model used in this study keeps the cognitive and meta-cognitive dimensions separate, unlike Thomas and Inkson's (2003) model.

Thomas and Inkson's (2003) original model was highly business-oriented and focused on managers within organizations doing business globally; however, the authors broadened the scope of their model in 2009 to incorporate interactions on a personal level outside of organizational business situations within the same cultural intelligence components (Thomas & Inkson, 2009). Both variations of the model are relevant, but not used in this study primarily because the models lack any coverage of an individual's motivation. Given that motivation is a significant part of an individual's desire to enter the global marketplace, Thomas and Inkson's (2003, 2009) models were insufficient for the true breadth of this study.

With the individual-focused four-factor model dominating the understanding of cultural intelligence, Ang and Inkpen (2008) wanted to explore the relevance of these dimensions on an organizational scale. The authors developed a new framework for firm-level cultural intelligence that involved joined the individual and organizational elements of cultural intelligence into three general areas: managerial, competitive, and structural. The firm-level model was not used in the study for two reasons. First, the model is designed for organizational analysis rather than individual analysis, and would be disjointed with the individual-level data obtained for market orientation. Second, the model, although shown credible through cursory validation, has not been sufficiently validated with a broader set of business parameters. Currently, the area of firm-level cultural intelligence is lacking in peer-reviewed research, unlike the dynamically researched four-factor model.

Bucher (2008) took a slightly different approach and presented cultural intelligence as a culmination of three different individual competencies: cultural awareness, cultural understanding, and cultural intelligence skills. Bucher's (2008) model complements the individual competencies with nine distinct "megaskills" (p. 10) that were deemed necessary to have in the workplace. These are: understanding cultural identity, checking cultural lenses, having global consciousness, shifting perspectives, communicating cross-culturally, managing intercultural conflict, implementing multicultural teaming, dealing with bias, and understanding the dynamics of power (Bucher, 2008). Although the model presents an important set of skills to develop and maintain individual cultural intelligence, the model will not be used in this study. Bucher's model is qualitative and introduces subjectivity that does not offer the definitive boundaries needed for behavioral, physical, and cognitive abilities. The four-factor model is quantitative and measureable, and offers distinct boundaries for analysis. Varying again from the four-factor model, Bucher's model lacks significant focus on an individual's motivation to gain cultural intelligence. These gaps would not enable adequate analysis for this study.

Adding a different perspective to cultural intelligence, Plum (2008) developed a model variation for cultural intelligence that highlights behaviors, cultural understandings, and communicative skills of individuals. Plum's (2008) model, first published in Danish, ascribes three distinct dimensions to individual cultural intelligence, namely intercultural engagement, cultural understanding, and intercultural communication. For this study, Plum's model was not used because it lacks proper emphasis on motivational and metacognitive factors for a suitable analysis with market orientation and the global engineering market.

Perhaps the most similar variation to the four-factor model used in the study is Livermore's model for cultural intelligence. Like many of the models just discussed, Livermore (2010) focused his model on individuals as global leaders, but moved the concept of cultural intelligence as a set of dimensions that can be learned. This model is founded from Earley and Ang's (2003) concepts and, more directly, Ang, VanDyne, and Koh's (2006) four-factor model. The model has four distinct dimensions named CQ Drive, CQ Knowledge, CQ Strategy, and CQ Action (Livermore, 2010, 2011). Each dimension in the model is associated directly with a factor in the four-factor cultural intelligence model, namely *CQ Drive* is related to motivation, *CQ Knowledge* is related to cognition, *CQ Strategy* is related to meta-cognition, and *CQ Action* is related to behavior (Livermore, 2010, 2011).

Where Livermore's model differs is that this model is structured to serve as a four-step cycle to develop cultural intelligence. Each dimension serves as a step for reflection, individual capability assessment, and improvement identification. The model is highly focused on individuals as dynamic global leaders rather than organizational team members (Livermore, 2010). Although similar to the four-factor model, Livermore's model was not used in this study primarily because the focus of the study was quantitative analysis for a baseline correlation rather than Livermore's qualitative analysis of individual managers.

Four-Factor Model for Cultural Intelligence

Taking hints about the dichotomy of cognition from Earley and Ang's (2003) model, Earley and Peterson (2004) applied the model in the context of individual training, but formally broke up the cognition factor into two distinct factors: cognition (general thinking and knowledge about cultures) and metacognition (higher-level thinking about the concepts associated with cultural knowledge). Earley and Peterson's (2004) derivation of the earlier model has become the standard four-factor model for cultural intelligence, although Earley and Peterson (2004) admit that the earlier model has the framework of the four-factor model. Ang, VanDyne, and Koh (2006) followed suit and examined how personality traits can be significant predictors to the four factors of cultural intelligence.

Almost all research afterward referred to Earley and Ang's initial model as a four-factor framework, although some research, most notably Thomas (2006), still subsume both components under the original cognitive factor. Schaffer and Miller (2008) acknowledged the cognition dichotic definition and chose to examine cultural intelligence as a singular concept in relation to expatriates. Ang et al. (2007) formally operationalized the cultural intelligence model with metacognition as the fourth factor by developing precise measurements for cultural intelligence as it applies to cultural judgment, decision making, cultural adaptation, and general task performance. Understanding the definitive context of market orientation, this correlational research will use the more defined four-factor model as the theoretical basis for the study. Discussions of the model's four factors follow.

Metacognitive Cultural Intelligence. According to Ang et al. (2007), metacognitive cultural intelligence is an individual's awareness of other cultures, particularly during interactions with people of different cultural backgrounds. This factor characterizes an individual's thinking (mental) process in cross-cultural engagements. In fact, metacognitive cultural intelligence involves higher-level thinking (Ang et al., 2007; Ang & Van Dyne, 2008) and promotes dynamic thinking about the multifarious cultural backgrounds of different people (Van Dyne, Ang, & Koh, 2008). Livermore (2010) suggested that business leaders who have high metacognitive cultural intelligence are strategists who have the ability for robust cultural awareness, sound planning, and effective monitoring of cultural interactions.

Cognitive Cultural Intelligence. Van Dyne, Ang, and Koh (2008) defined cognitive cultural intelligence as "an individual's cultural knowledge of norms, practices, and conventions in different cultural settings" (p. 17). People with high cultural intelligence have individual knowledge of cross-cultural issues and variations, which proves vital to cross-cultural decision making and business performance (Van Dyne, Ang, & Koh, 2008). The cognitive factor encompasses knowledge of different cultures from business customs and economic systems to social structures and cultural values (Ang et al., 2007). This factor is particularly knowledge-based and involves understanding cultural variances, recognizing how culture molds business practices, and ascertaining cultural values (Livermore, 2010). Cognitive cultural intelligence is a desirable trait for global business leaders. Ang and Van Dyne (2008) summarized that individuals with high cognitive cultural intelligence are better prepared and able for cross-cultural exchanges.

Behavioral Cultural Intelligence. Behavioral cultural intelligence is an individual's ability to act appropriately in cross-cultural situations, particularly through verbal and nonverbal actions (Livermore, 2010). Leaders with high behavioral cultural intelligence will know how to conduct interactions appropriately with people from differing cultural backgrounds, including knowing what to say and how to say it. Ang et al. (2007) explained that appropriate behaviors include culturally suitable words, mannerisms, expressions, and vocal tone. Individuals with high cultural intelligence are mindful of the impressions their actions make during cross-cultural interactions, and critically aware that their behaviors may alter the perceptions and responses of their culturally-diverse counterparts (Rogers, 2008). Ultimately, behavioral cultural intelligence is the model's component that is established through individual action.

Motivational Cultural Intelligence. Motivational cultural intelligence is the ability to drive individual learning about cultural differences and provide focus on cross-cultural situations (Ang et al., 2007; Ang & Van Dyne, 2008). This factor involves the motivation to adapt cross-culturally and apply energy to overcoming cultural challenges (Livermore, 2010). Van Dyne, Ang, and Koh (2008) suggested that motivational cultural intelligence is a unique form of self-efficacy that evokes confidence and individual interest in different cultural situations. Individuals with high motivational cultural intelligence are energetic and highly motivated to serve as active participants in the multi-cultural environment.

Cultural Intelligence Scale (CQS)

As discussed earlier, the four-factor model constitutes the cultural intelligence-focused theoretical basis for this study. As a quantitative measure of cultural intelligence, Van Dyne, Ang, and Koh (2008) validated the Cultural Intelligence Scale (CQS), which was based on the four-factor model and initial CQS validation work of Ang et al. (2007). The CQS is a 20-item scale used for the self-assessment and peer-assessment of cultural intelligence levels, both on a cumulative level and on an individual factor level (Van Dyne, Ang, & Koh, 2008).

The CQS was a logical selection for use in this study because the theoretical framework is partially based on the Earley and Ang's (2003) model of cultural intelligence and the quantitative study will require a valid measurement of cultural intelligence as a whole and among its factors. The scale items have strong psychometric properties, comprising four items for metacognitive measurement, six items for cognitive measurement, five items for motivational measurement, and five items for behavioral measurement (Ang et al., 2007; Van Dyne, Ang, & Koh, 2008).

Cultural Intelligence and Organizational Performance

Cultural intelligence has become a significant factor in effective performance on both the individual and organizational levels (Amiri, Moghimi, & Kazemi, 2010). Research indicates that culturally intelligent individuals prompt positive organizational performance when conducting business or other activities across country borders (Earley & Peterson, 2004). Likewise, organizations that make cultural intelligence a priority in their business strategy experience such benefits as enhanced performance, better decision making, flexibility, and international expansion (Livermore, 2010). Consequently, cultural intelligence influences an organization's performance on many levels.

Research has shown that cultural intelligence within organizations proves a valid predictor to the organization's cultural judgment and decision making (Ng, Tan, & Ang, 2011) and supports the effectiveness of expatriates on staff (Kim, Kirkman, & Chen, 2008; Templar, Tay, & Chandrasekar, 2006). This individual effectiveness better positions organizations for global, culturally-diverse environments (Lovvorn &Chen, 2011). Adding to this understanding, Oolders, Chernyshenko, and Stark (2008) posited that individuals who were open to new experiences had higher cultural intelligence and enhanced the likelihood of other adaptive performance abilities. Culturally intelligent leaders influence the organization and positively affect the organization's collective ability to understand diverse customers, conduct activities to enhance cultural perspectives, and adapt to different environments for job performance success (Livermore, 2010).

Part of an organization's performance is reaching economic goals.

Waclawski (2002) argued that there exists a notable association between perceived cultural flexibility (openness) and financial performance. In studying small businesses in Canada, de la Garza-Carranza and Egri (2010) stated that although cultural intelligence was positively related to corporate reputation and employee commitment, financial performance was not positively affected. These conflicting accounts suggest that cultural intelligence is not a solitary factor in any organization's success, but provides positive impacts on the organization's overall performance and mission.

Cultural intelligence has become an important business consideration within organizations. Bucher (2008) suggested that cultural intelligence serves as an organizational bottom-line issue, influencing organizational success, productivity, client relationships, and operational existence in the marketplace. In fact, cultural intelligence stems from individual leaders and spreads throughout the organization (Bucher, 2008). Culturally intelligent leaders who have satisfactory leadership and interpersonal skills will enhance the organization's ability to succeed in the global marketplace (Creque & Gooden, 2011). Similarly, Livermore (2010) contends that organizations that incorporate cultural intelligence as part of their business process are likely to fulfill their organizational mission and achieve desired organizational performance goals.

Market Orientation

Market orientation has been a staple in business practice over the past six decades through a conceptual evolution starting from the marketing concept and notions of customer orientation to the current selection of market orientation models (Tomášková, 2009). This evolution of concept begot various different understandings of market orientation that developed into robust market orientation models and business practices. In this chapter, popular definitions and models used in research are reviewed. The specific firm-level models discussed include Kohli and Jaworski's (1990) market orientation model, Narver and Slater's (1990) market orientation model, and Deshpandé, Farley, and Webster (1993) customer orientation model. Other firm-level models are also briefly covered. Individual market orientation and the I-MARKOR scale, both used in this study, are detailed. The coverage of various models lead into the relevant topics of global market orientation and the cultural aspects of market orientation. Both topics have direct connections to this study and offer associations to cultural intelligence and the global engineering marketplace. Concluding this section is a discussion of the influence of market orientation on organizational performance.

The Evolution of Market Orientation

The principles of market orientation have existed in the business realm since the 1950s and through the years, the definition of market orientation has evolved but not without conflicting perspectives and differing approaches (Tomášková, 2009). Market orientation has been referred to by various monikers, beginning as *the marketing concept* and transforming into *marketing orientation, customer orientation,* and *market orientation.* Different perspectives exist for the differences in meaning of each; however, for the intent of this research, these monikers are used interchangeably.

Market orientation is a complex concept that goes beyond understanding the customer or market. Johnson (1998) stated that market orientation focuses on both clientele and business competition in the marketplace with regard to business strategy, decision making, and market understanding. This premise has remained steadfast throughout the evolution of market orientation from the early perspectives of the marketing concept to the multiplicity of valid models used in current research. Felton (1959) started this conceptual progression with the marketing concept described as "a corporate state of mind that insists on the integration and coordination of all of the marketing functions which, in turn, are melded with other corporate functions, for the basic objective of producing maximum long-range corporate profits" (p. 55). Felton's marketing-focused approach to business strategy was revolutionary to corporate business functions, products, and profitability. Levitt (1960) introduced the idea of a customer-oriented company and highlighted that organizational leaders need not focus on selling products, but rather focus on buying customers. McNamara (1972) joined the ideas of the marketing concept and customer orientation and emphasized the importance of market-based communication.

Throughout the 1970s and most of the 1980s, the broader variations of the marketing concept and customer orientation were researched and used in business practice, which further advanced the conceptual path to market orientation. Shapiro (1988) and Webster (1988) were the first to conceptualize and detail characteristics of a market-oriented firm. Shapiro (1988) characterized market-oriented firms as recognizing no difference between being market driven and being customer oriented. Webster (1988), who clearly shared Shapiro's (1988) viewpoints, reinforced the significance of a strong focus on business profitability and customer best interests. Trustrum (1989) took this idea further and suggested that market-oriented firms should not only strive for customer satisfaction, but should also strive to suitably align the market needs to the firm's true capabilities.

The historical perspectives have laid the groundwork for current definitions and models of market orientation, including popular models such as Narver and Slater's (1990); Kohli and Jaworski's (1990); and Deshpandé, Farley, and Webster (1993) models. According to Stoelhorst and van Raaij (2004), both Narver and Slater's (1990) and Kohli and Jaworski's (1990) definitions of market orientation are the two most prominent used in research. The following subsections describe these prominent models as well as the advancement to an individual-level perspective of market orientation.

Prominent Models of Market Orientation

Narver and Slater's Market Orientation Model. Narver and Slater's (1990) perspectives transformed the existing business understanding of market orientation to one that involved internal behaviors that directly affected the external-focused service. Narver and Slater (1990) defined market orientation as "the organization culture that most effectively and efficiently creates the necessary behaviors for the creation of superior value for buyers and, thus, continuous superior performance for the business" (p. 21). From this viewpoint, Narver and Slater (1990) developed a market orientation model based on three behavioral components: customer orientation, competitor orientation, and interfunctional coordination. Customer orientation relates to an adequate understanding of a client or market base to provide premium service reliably. Competitor orientation relates to understanding competitor strengths and weaknesses in conjunction with their overall business strategy and service competences. The third behavioral component, interfunctional coordination, involves a firm's collective use of resources to provide premium, reliable service to customers (Narver & Slater, 1990).

The Narver and Slater (1990) model had limitations with regard to the study and measurement of market orientation. This model was not used in the research study for two specific reasons. First, like the predecessor constructs, the model was focused on organizational behaviors rather than the variant behaviors of the individuals making up the organization (Schlosser & McNaughton, 2009). Because of the firm-level design, this model only offered one perspective per organization and failed to allow discernment of any multi-layered employee perspective. Second, the Narver and Slater (1990) model and its available scale, called the MKTOR scale, have a lack of dimension. According to Gauzente (1999), the model and its measurement do not account for any cultural or stakeholder dimensions of market orientation. Tomášková (2009) clarified that the model's measurement only provides insight into two stakeholder orientations: customers and competitors. Both areas of insight had minimal value for the purpose of this research study.

Kohli and Jaworski's Market Orientation. Kohli and Jaworski's (1990) model for market orientation was published around the same time as Narver and Slater's model, but had a stronger focus on cultural aspects within an organization. The model was based on Kohli and Jaworski's (1990) definition of market orientation as "the organizationwide *generation* of market intelligence pertaining to current and future customer needs, *dissemination* of the intelligence across departments, and organizationwide *responsiveness* to it" (p. 6). The behavioral elements of this perspective of market orientation were like that of Narver and Slater's (1990) perspective, but with stronger emphasis on how the firms interact with and respond to the marketplace. Gauzente (1999) stated that both models were very similar; however, Kohli and Jaworski's (1990) model had a significant cultural element.

The model focused on three components: intelligence generation, intelligence dissemination, and responsiveness (Kohli & Jaworski, 1990, 1993; Kohli, Jaworski & Kumar, 1993). *Intelligence generation* refers to the acquisition and assessment of market information, particularly customer requirements. *Intelligence dissemination* refers to the sharing of market and customer information within an organization. Responsiveness refers to the actions taken in response to market information (Kohli & Jaworski, 1990, 1993; Kohli, Jaworski & Kumar, 1993). As a method to quantify an organization's level of market orientation, Kohli, Jaworski and Kumar (1993) developed the MARKOR scale to measure an organization's capability for the model's three components. The scale that was used in this research study, the I-MARKOR scale, was directly based on Kohli, Jaworski and Kumar's (1993) original, firm-level MARKOR scale.

Important to this study was the fact that Jaworski and Kohli (1993) expanded their earlier definition of market orientation by redefining the responsiveness factor of market orientation to two distinct components: response design and response implementation. Aided by their research, which focused on the antecedents and consequences to market orientation, Jaworski and Kohli (1993) refined the MARKOR items by separating the 14 responsiveness items into the expanded components of response design and response implementation. The expanded components in the firm-level scale provided the developmental foundation for the individual-level scale that will be used for this research study. The refinement of market-oriented responsiveness aided future research in understanding the distinctions in business responses to markets.

However standard in research and business use, the Jaworski and Kohli (1993) model was not used for this research study for two reasons. First, the model was limited to organization-wide representation of market orientation and failed to adequately reflect differences within an organization's rank of employees. According to Schlosser and McNaughton (2009), the model and its measured application only offer a single perception of market orientation and do not reflect the differences in customer-oriented activities amongst the senior, middle, and junior level employees. Through this model, an organization's competitor advantage relies upon customer-oriented services offered by the range of employees in the company and not just the upper echelon of management (Schlosser & McNaughton, 2009). Understanding market-oriented activities of different managers was a significant element of this research study for which the Jaworski and Kohli (1993) model did not offer.

Second, Kohli, Jaworski, and Kumar (1993) suggested that the available scale for the model, the MARKOR, was not generalizable across all industries. An important element of this research study was the ability to measure market orientation and have it generalizable globally, across all engineering disciplines and industries. The Jaworski and Kohli (1993) model and its measurement did not offer the necessary generalizability across the study's population to provide valid determinations.

Deshpandé, Farley, and Webster (1993) Customer Orientation Model. After the notable research from Kohli and Jaworski (1990), Jaworski and Kohli (1993), and Narver and Slater (1990), there existed soaring interest in market orientation and renewed interest in the marketing concept, particularly with relation to customer orientation and business performance (Hadcroft & Jarratt, 2007; Tomášková, 2009). Deshpandé, Farley, and Webster (1993) recognized this trend and developed a revised definition of customer orientation (used synonymously with market orientation) that drew closer to understanding individual perspectives. Deshpandé, Farley, and Webster (1993) defined customer orientation as "the set of beliefs that puts the customer's interest first, while not excluding those of all other stakeholders such as owners, managers, and employees, in order to develop a long-term profitable enterprise" (p. 27). This definition served as the conceptual basis for Deshpandé, Farley, and Webster's (1993) popular research in Japan using 138 in-country executives to relate customer orientation, innovation, and organizational culture as associated with business performance. Supporting their new definition of customer orientation (market orientation), the authors developed a customer orientation scale to measure the customer orientation, culture, innovativeness, and performance (Deshpandé & Farley, 1998; Deshpandé, Farley & Webster, 1993).

The reemergence of the customer orientation perspective brought fresh ideas to the rising concept of market orientation and figuratively paved a path to future research on customer and market-focused orientation. As example, Johnson (1998) delineated the concept of customer orientation with regard to market orientation and total quality management to develop new perspectives and measurements for customer satisfaction and quality improvement.

For this study, the Customer Orientation model was not used. First, the model, however open to multiple management perspectives, had a firm-level focus and used the collective accounting of the management perspectives. This research study maintained focus on the individual-level perspective only. Second, the model did not adequately facilitate measurement of how market information was acquired or disseminated. The model's scale measured on a cursory level the general market intelligence. Lastly, the model did not address or facilitate measurement of market orientation as related to a response to market information. Ultimately, Deshpandé, Farley, and Webster's (1993) Customer Orientation model was not sufficient for the purposes of this study.

Other Firm-Level Models and Instruments. The early market orientation models and scales have served as the foundation for current research, perspectives, and measurement of market orientation relative to many different facets of business, industry, and application. Various firm-level models and instruments have been developed based upon the Kohli and Jaworski (1990), Jaworski and Kohli (1993), and Narver and Slater (1990) models; however, these alternate models and measurement instruments have been specifically designed to meet the needs of distinct markets and businesses. For example, Deng and Dart's (1994) model incorporates business prosperity on Jaworski and Kohli's (1993) model; Lado, Maydeu-Olivares, and Rivera's (1998) model focuses on stakeholders; and Farrell and Oczkowski's (1998) model tries to bridge MKTOR and MARKOR (Tomášková, 2009).

Tomášková (2009) outlined 26 different methods to measure market orientation; however, these scales have shortcomings. Since these different scales are developed using the MKTOR or MARKOR measure, the variant scales are generally focused on organizational rather than individual behaviors related to customers, competition, and cooperation (Schlosser & McNaughton, 2009; Tomášková, 2009). Relative to this study, these scales, and the models they are based on, offered but one perspective per organization and failed to capture any multidimensional employee perspective.

Tomášková (2009) stated another shortcoming to these scales is that they contain items that are the results of and not components of market orientation, such as business performance and new product success. This injection of business consequences into the market orientation concept overshadows some components of market orientation or causes some components to be missed altogether in the measurement (Tomášková, 2009). For this research, all components of market orientation needed to be represented and measured effectively.

The merits to an individual-level focus on market orientation have been gaining attention in the research community. Schlosser's (2004) research on the market-oriented contributions of individuals broke new ground in the understanding of the human behavioral components associated with customer and market interaction. Schlosser's research led to an individual-level model, based on Jaworski and Kohli's (1993) model, and a construct based on the MARKOR scale, called the I-MARKOR, described in the next subsection. Rather than measuring one collective perspective from an organization, the individual-level construct offers a window into multiple perspectives from an organization and exposes important subtle and not so subtle differentiations in viewpoint within a single organization (Schlosser & McNaughton, 2009).

Individual Market Orientation and the I-MARKOR Scale. Schlosser (2004) advanced the research focus of market orientation from the traditional firm-level vantage to an individual-level construct through recognition of the important and diverse individual perspectives. The concept of individual market orientation is a relatively fresh branch of market orientation research. Zhu (2011) acknowledged that individual market orientation is sparsely studied in literature. Ho, Niden, and Johneny (2011) stated that much of the existing literature on market orientation has focused on the organizational level and has lacked in the establishment of contribution of individuals. Although understudied, the employee (individual) perspectives with regard to market orientation can expose the differences in perspectives within the same organization and expose the variant contributions to the collective organizational viewpoint.

Lings and Greenley (2010) suggested that individual attitudes and behaviors within an organization can influence the organization's market orientation; however, they also acknowledged a lack of understanding with regard to influences on strategic direction, such as a marketing response to market information. Regarding professional service firms, Tschida (2010) stated that strategic, relationship-based marketing is more robust on the individual-level, as opposed to the organizational-level. Moreover, Ho, Niden, and Johneny (2011) studied and measured individual market orientation elements within the financial sector to understand the pertinent individual behaviors essential to improving individual performance. These individual behaviors affect strategic decisions and direction at organizations. According to Lings and Greenley (2010), individuals (employees) who are market oriented in their job functions will naturally align with the strategic flow of the organization. These individual behaviors will likely be a positive influence on the organization (Lings & Greenley, 2010).

To understand the benefits of individual marketing orientation, the historical models and measurements of market orientation, which is firm-based only, prove insufficient. Correct characterization and measurement of individual market orientation required a new model and a reliable individual-level scale. Based on the germinal work of Kohli and Jaworski (1990) and Jaworski and Kohli (1993), Schlosser (2004) developed an individual model for market orientation that transfigures the three firm-level components of Kohli and Jaworski's (1990) model to three similar individual level components. Schlosser's (2004) model identifies the information acquisition, information sharing, and strategic response capacity of individual decision makers (Ho, Niden, & Johneny, 2011; Schlosser, 2004; Schlosser & McNaughton, 2009).

Schlosser (2004) stated that her model's *information acquisition* component, which is related directly to Kohli and Jaworski's (1990) intelligence generation dimension, characterizes how individuals obtain and assess market information. The model's *information sharing* component, which is directly related to Kohli and Jaworski's (1990) intelligence dissemination dimension, involves how an individual disseminates and distributes market information. This individual trait has links to an individual's communication abilities and flexibility (Schlosser & McNaughton, 2009). The model's last component, *strategic response*, is linked to Kohli and Jaworski's (1990) responsiveness dimension and characterizes how an individual uses market information to develop market-specific strategies (Schlosser, 2004; Schlosser & McNaughton, 2009). A significant factor for using Schlosser's (2004) market orientation model in this study aside from the individual-level construct was that the model was based on a reliable and well-researched market orientation construct.

To measure the level of individual market orientation wholly and by its components, Schlosser and McNaughton (2009) developed and validated the I-MARKOR scale. Based on Kohli, Jaworski, and Kumar's (1993) 20-item scale, the I-MARKOR scale reveals individual differences in market orientation and can be implemented across different industries. According to Schlosser and McNaughton (2009), the scale items characterize individual market-oriented behaviors that render to different professionals and different work functions. The scale can be used to distinguish best market-oriented practices and measure dynamic individual capabilities (Schlosser & McNaughton, 2009). This scale was ideal for the current study because of the individual-level construct and the sample population variation with regard to engineering organization size, market perspectives, marketing response, and the global market motivation. The I-MARKOR offered the flexibility to adequately measure market orientation from this varied group of participants.

Global Market Orientation

Global market orientation (also known as *international market orientation*) is a step beyond general market orientation in that behaviors are focused on the current needs of, anticipated future needs of, and competition within the international marketplace (Monferrer, Blesa, & Ripollés, 2012). In fact, global market orientation is considered a precursor to globalization (Monferrer, Blesa, & Ripollés, 2012). Organizations and individuals focused on the international marketplace can benefit from applying market-oriented behaviors to their global business targets and bridge new multicultural connections.

Resembling the industry particulars and multiple definitions of market orientation, global market orientation holds different meanings for different individuals, organizations, and markets. Decision makers must recognize their global goals (Fung, Fung, & Wind, 2008). Tung and Miller (1990) stated that developing a global market orientation is imperative for business leaders, particularly to define international and domestic competition, determine relationships within target markets, and respond to the customer's needs wherever that customer is headquartered. Determining what a global market orientation means to organizations is a difficult task for individuals; however, the results of this understanding are significantly positive for organizational performance and decision making (Tung & Miller, 1990).

Global orientation requires support and commitment from employees and organizational leadership alike. Diamantopoulos and Cadogan (1996) examined global market orientation from the context of exporters and found that prominent firm-wide market orientation behaviors were the result of heightened coordination among individuals and decision makers within the organization. Global market-oriented behaviors play a significant role in developing and enhancing cross-cultural relationships (Osayomi, 2007). Cross-cultural relationships can positively affect international performance and market success. Tung and Miller (1990) suggested that without such commitment to global orientation, the results can be detrimental to the ultimate sustainability and success of the organization.

Market information acquisition and dissemination concerning the global business landscape is an asset to companies trying to enter global markets. Monferrer, Blesa, and Ripollés (2012) stated that these global market-oriented behaviors are pivotal in obtaining international market intelligence and accelerate how organizational decision makers use this market intelligence to add to their organization's internal knowledgebase. Individuals who exhibit these market-oriented behaviors are undoubtedly assets to their organizations and serve as international barometers. Specifically, globally-oriented managers have a dynamic understanding of the international marketplace and can easily identify changes in different global markets (Monferrer, Blesa, & Ripollés, 2012). Consequently, this understanding facilitates adaptation to the changes and shifting customer needs, as well as to different global environments and cultures (Monferrer,

Blesa, & Ripollés, 2012; Nummela, Saarenketo, & Puumalainen, 2004).

Although not yet fully explored, individual global market orientation and intelligence can provide enormous benefits to companies trying to break into new international markets. Individuals placed within the front lines of the global marketplace, for example, provides valuable information to the organization and adds significant knowledge to the company's global market knowledgebase (Monferrer, Blesa, & Ripollés, 2012; Tichy & DeRose, 2006). Individual knowledge through expatriation has served as a valuable tool for global market orientation development and international relationship building (Boyacigiller, 1991). Adding valued individual knowledge enhances and benefits the organization's collective global market orientation behaviors.

Of particular importance to this study, globally-focused market-oriented firms can subdue cultural distance problems, which can surface as elements of risk or uncertainty, information consistency, or disreputable behavior (Monferrer, Blesa, & Ripollés, 2012). Global market orientation involves flexibility, awareness, competence and being proactive (Nummela, Saarenketo, & Puumalainen, 2004). Consequently, globally-focused market-oriented behaviors can minimize risk and uncertainty through a heightened understanding of the target market and the cultural norms to doing business in that market (Monferrer, Blesa, & Ripollés, 2012). This heightened awareness can also facilitate more consistency with how information is acquired and disseminated, particularly better communication between the cultures, and summarily minimize any problems surfacing from the cultural distance. Weick and Sutcliffe (2007) stated that lacking mindfulness in any form of business conduct exposes the blunders of mismanaged unknowns and impedes dependable and consistent business performance. Globally-focused market orientation can also counter any disreputable or opportunistic behavior through better awareness of the marketplace and business process (Monferrer, Blesa, & Ripollés, 2012). Global market orientation enhances cross-cultural relationships and helps nullify cultural boundaries (Osayomi, 2007). Ultimately, individual and organization leaders' actions, such as remaining mindful of the unknowns, conducting marketplace needs assessments, and supporting expatriation, are beneficial to understanding different cultures, business environments, and performance impacts.

Cultural Aspects of Market Orientation

Detailed from the early frameworks of market orientation, culture has played a significant role in organizational and individual market-focused behaviors. Narver and Slater (1990) developed their market orientation framework from a cultural context rather than the managerial context of the predecessor marketing concept frameworks. The authors related the organization's culture to the market-oriented qualities of the firm, specifically customer orientation, competitor orientation, and interfunctional coordination. Even though there is recognition of the role of internal organizational culture in market orientation, researchers have not considered how market orientation is related to external cultures with regard to market and locale. The cultural factors of a market are often discounted by decision makers, but serve as excellent points of origin to understanding a customer's core needs and belief systems (Johnson, 1998). Sanzo, Santos, Vázquez, and Álvarez (2003) suggested the existence of culturally-influenced market orientation and indicated a direct relationship to a firm's collective ability to maintain longstanding customer relationships and achieve customer loyalty.

Market orientation behaviors are directly influenced by the organizational leadership and environment. According to Hult, Snow, and Kandemir (2003), key components of market-oriented behaviors, such as customer and competitor alignments, and internal coordination, are directly influenced by organizational leadership and decision maker cultural alignments. Consequently, the organization's competitiveness is enriched by these individual market-oriented behaviors (Hult et al., 2003). Mavondo and Farrell (2003) looked at culture from a cultural orientation context and found that organizational leaders that respond to market needs with a consensual outward-focus within their organizations experience more enhanced marketing and fiscal performance.

Effective individual market orientations involve leader awareness of various markets and national cultures. According to Alexander and Wilson (1997), global decision makers need to be leaders across cultures and cognizant of the differences in people and business environments. Brettel, Engelen, Heinemann, and Vadhanasindhu (2008) examined the cultural aspects of market orientation behavior and found that management approaches that work in the United States and throughout the Americas do not necessarily work elsewhere in the world. They asserted that the cultural implications of successful decision making encompass individual cultural dispositions and alignments. In sum, developing a keen understanding of market and organizational cultures can positively affect the organization's bottom-line and overarching performance.

Market Orientation and Organizational Performance

Firms use market orientation to delineate better solutions expressly to meet the needs of the market and customers. Similar to cultural intelligence, the presence of market-oriented behaviors within an organization adds value to the organization's market performance. Much research has been conducted empirically finding that market-oriented behaviors improve an organization's performance (Cano, Carrillat, &

Jaramillo, 2004; Ceyhan, 2004; Deshpandé, Farley, & Webster, 1993; Jaworski & Kohli, 1993; Kara, Spillan, & DeShields, 2005; Narver & Slater, 1990, 1999; Ruekert, 1992). There exists research showing a negative or null relationship between market orientation and performance; however, those studies are vastly in the minority over the portfolio of research showing a markedly positive relationship (Cano, Carrillat, & Jaramillo, 2004). Market orientation has also been proven highly beneficial and important to an organization's market competitiveness and fiscal performance (Schlosser & McNaughton, 2009). Cano, Carrillat, and Jaramillo (2004) added that market orientation is a significant precursor to organization-wide performance and, if maintained within an organization, can create market longevity and sustainable success.

Market orientation supports the recognition of customer needs and market service gaps, which are vital to optimal financial and operational performance. Kohli and Jaworski (1990) stated that market-oriented firms generally experience higher customer satisfaction; employee satisfaction and commitment; and business performance. Market differentiation can fill service gaps through innovative solutions. Cano, Carrillat, and Jaramillo (2004) suggested that service differentiation in tandem with market-oriented behaviors mark the top two drivers for business performance, while Vázquez, Santos, and Álvarez (2001) suggested that market orientation has positive impact on a firm's ability to develop and foster innovation. Innovation can undoubtedly influence business performance and, according to Olavarrieta and Friedmann (2008), is the most important resource firms have to promote positive business performance.

Conclusion

Evidenced by the in-depth research review, market-oriented behaviors and culturally-intelligent behaviors independently add value to an organization's performance and marketplace success. Both cultural intelligence and market orientation are well-studied concepts and play an integral part in business profitability (Narver & Slater, 1999; Scholl, 2009; Vytlacil; 2010). Although, individually, these two concepts are well studied and offer value to an organization, the relationship (if any) that exists between market-oriented and culturally intelligent behaviors is unknown. Understanding this relationship may support positive spread into global markets. In the context of U.S. country of origin engineering firms, individual decision makers and leaders can embrace cultural intelligence and market orientation within their own behaviors to prompt positive organizational performance and enhance cross-cultural relationships when conducting business across country borders (Earley & Peterson, 2004; Osayomi, 2007).

Promoting behaviors that reflect cultural intelligence and market orientation within corporations requires leadership commitment. Tung and Miller (1990) suggested that leadership commitment to global market orientation can result in enhancements in organization's sustainability and success. Likewise, organizations that make cultural intelligence a priority in their business strategy experience such benefits as enhanced performance, better decision making, flexibility, and international expansion (Livermore, 2010). Global leaders can ultimately benefit from market-oriented and culturally-intelligent behaviors by facilitating better decision making.

Advancing the concepts of market orientation and cultural intelligence to the global stage is becoming a necessity for sustainability among engineering firms, particularly given that once domestic-only firms now compete globally to stay economically balanced and survive (Acosta et al., 2010). Engineering decision makers are realizing they need to develop a global perspective (Valenti, 1995). Globally-oriented, culturally-intelligent managers have a dynamic understanding of the international marketplace and can easily identify changes in different global markets (Monferrer, Blesa, & Ripollés, 2012) and form lasting cross-cultural relationships (Osayomi, 2007).

Recognizing any relationships between market orientation and cultural intelligence may ultimately serve as a tool for business sustainability, particularly through individual awareness of global decision maker behaviors. The literature review exposed a lack of empirical research associating cultural intelligence and market orientation to engineering design firms facing the global marketplace. Numerous past studies examined the relationship between culture and market orientation in the contexts of leadership behaviors and globalization. Studies included, among others, Nakata and Sivakumar (2001); Yaprak (2008); and Cadogan, Kuivalainen, and Sundqvist (2009). Further past studies analyzed cultural intelligence as it relates to different individual leader behaviors and performance, including Dean (2007); Scholl (2009); de la Garza-Carranza and Egri (2010); and numerous others. No empirical research exists that examines the relationship between cultural intelligence and market orientation in general or as related to engineering firms entering the global marketplace. An understanding of this relationship may support positive business expansion into global markets and promote business sustainability through global market engagement. An individual's awareness of their cultural intelligence and global market orientation skills will support their firm's shared and informed decisions regarding entry into the global marketplace (Hansen et al., 2011; Livermore, 2010). This heightened awareness can progress domestic engineering decision makers into globally-oriented, culturally-intelligent leaders. This study filed a gap in the existing research.

Summary

Chapter 2 incorporated a comprehensive literature review of the study's variables, cultural intelligence and market orientation, with research covering historical and current perspectives. While providing a full understanding of the study's primary topics, the chapter included discussions about the variables with regard to the concepts of and impacts on organizational performance and marketplace success. These discussions unveiled an evolution of the basic business constructs to the global marketplace. Beginning with an overview of the research process, the discussion offered a quantification of peer reviewed title, article, journal, and other multi-media literature searches.

The literature review was focused on two main topics: cultural intelligence and market orientation. The cultural intelligence literature review began with an analysis of the historical perspectives. These research documents included germinal studies on human intelligence, from psychometric models to multiple intelligences theory, the relationship between culture and intelligence, and the predominant cultural models. The cultural intelligence literature review also covered current perspectives, containing the predominantly used current models of cultural intelligence, specifically Earley and Ang's (2003) four-factor model which was used in this study. The chapter covered the generally positive relationship between cultural intelligence and organizational performance, both operational and financial. Lastly, the discussion included the multi-dimensional Cultural Intelligence Scale, which was used for this study.

The literature related to market orientation proved just as robust as the cultural intelligence research, and involved discussions of historical and current perspectives. The historical perspective discussion detailed germinal research including popular market orientation models and various approaches to traditional market orientation measurement. The discussion on current perspectives offered an array of models for organizational and individual market orientation including Schlosser's (2004) individual market orientation model, which will be a foundational concept in this study. The reviewed research included an examination of the cultural aspects of market orientation, which ranged from organizational culture to market cultures. Adding to the understanding of market orientation, the concept of global market orientation was examined through a review of recent studies on the subject. Completing the discussion is an analysis of the positive relationship between market orientation and organizational performance.

The chapter concluded with a discussion about how leaders and decision makers at U.S.-based engineering firms can embrace cultural intelligence and market orientation within their own behaviors and business interactions. Both cultural intelligence and market orientation are well-studied concepts and play an integral part in business profitability (Narver

& Slater, 1999; Scholl, 2009; Vytlacil; 2010). Taking these concepts to the global stage is becoming a necessity for sustainability among engineering firms, particularly given that once domestic-only firms now compete globally to stay economically balanced and survive (Acosta et al., 2010). As discovered in the literature review, decision makers who identify and use cultural intelligence with a global market orientation can potentially enhance their ability to enter the global engineering marketplace.

Through the literature review, gaps in the predecessor research were exposed. No empirical research exists that examines the relationship between cultural intelligence and market orientation as related to engineering firms entering the global marketplace. There exist past studies that have covered links between culture and market orientation, and cultural intelligence and different individual leader behaviors and performance. Although the past research provided background information for this study, the specific relationship between cultural intelligence and market orientation was unknown. This research study filled a literature gap.

In Chapter 3, the focus advanced from discussions of existing research literature and documentation that supported the basis for this study to a thorough discussion of the research approach and structure. The next chapter contains details about the appropriateness of the study's research design along with supporting information about the study's population, sampling frame, sampling approach, and the mitigation of threats to internal and external validity. The research design resulted in the quantifiable validation of every aggregate and subfactor relationship that exists between the cultural intelligence and market orientation of decision makers at U.S.-based engineering firms entering the global marketplace.

THREE

RESEARCH METHODOLOGY

The purpose of this quantitative correlational study was to determine any relationship between the independent variables of cultural intelligence and market orientation of decision makers at U.S.-based engineering firms to the dependent variable of entering the global marketplace. The Cultural Intelligence Scale (Ang et al., 2007; Van Dyne, Ang, & Koh, 2009) was used to measure the variable of cultural intelligence. The I-MARKOR (Schlosser, 2004; Schlosser & McNaughton, 2009) was used to measure the variable of market orientation. The study sample included senior-level global engineering and marketing decision makers from U.S.-based engineering firms listed on ENR's Top 150 Global Design Firms and Top 200 International Design Firms listings.

Chapter 3 includes information about this study's population, sampling frame, geographic location, informed consent, confidentiality, instrumentation, data collection, data retention and destruction, validity, reliability, and data analysis. Most importantly, the chapter includes justification for the research method and appropriateness of the research design. The section on instrumentation provides important confirmation regarding the reliability and validation of each instrument used in the study. The data analysis section offers insight into the descriptive and correlation analysis that was used to determine if significant relationships exist between cultural intelligence and global market orientation.

Research Method and Design Appropriateness

This research study involved a quantitative research method to understand relationships between cultural intelligence and market orientation within domestic engineering firms aimed at the global marketplace. A quantitative method was appropriate because it supported the characterization of trends or relationships among two or more variables and the precision measurement of these relationships (Cooper & Schindler, 2003). A primary aim of this study was to precisely understand the variable relationships, if any. A qualitative research method is exploratory (Cooper & Schindler, 2003) and did not provide any degree of precision measurement or analysis necessary to conduct the study. A quantitative method involves statistical analysis and comparison of numerical or categorical data gathered from any mix of surveys, interviews, observations, and document analyses (Symonds & Gorard, 2010). This study involved the use of two quantifiable surveys (CQS and I-MARKOR) from which statistical analyses and comparisons was performed.

This study's primary focus was to recognize any influences or relationships the two variables, cultural intelligence and market orientation, have on each other. A correlational design was used for this study because the two variables have an unknown influence on each other when related to U.S. engineering firms competing globally. Use of a correlational research design involved correlation statistical testing to determine the degree of relationship between two or more variables (Salkind, 2003). This research design was appropriate for this study because the variables had an undetermined relationship and the research design permitted statistical validation for or against any influence or relationship.

According to Johnson and Christenson (2012), correlational research is appropriate when the variables of interest are quantitative. This study's design enabled a variety of statistical analyses of the collected quantitative data from participant responses. Descriptive statistical analysis and the calculation of Spearman's rho (ρ) coefficient provided calculable evidence of any relationship that might exist between the variables. Correlation analysis enabled determination if significant linear relationships existed between cultural intelligence and market orientation (Triola, 2005). The correlation coefficient and resulting correlational matrix disclosed the correlation's strength, direction, and degree of association (Chen & Popovich, 2002; Cooper & Schindler, 2003).

This correlational study had an explanatory design to highlight any relationship that existed between cultural intelligence and market orientation in the context of global-bound U.S. engineering firms. An explanatory correlational research design was used to help relate different variables, either on a one-to-one or one-to-many basis (Chen & Popovich, 2002; Salkind, 2003). This study detailed relations of each dimension of cultural intelligence to each dimension of market orientation, which presented a one-to-many research scenario. Other designs were considered but found inadequate for this study. A quasi-experimental or true experimental design, for example, would have involved the control of some or all of the variables (Neuman, 2006; Salkind, 2003); however, the variables of cultural intelligence and market orientation were uncontrollable because they were distinct to each participant. Exploratory and descriptive designs did not fit this study's parameters, since both designs could only help in illuminating the roles of the variables. This research was not intended to further clarify the variables, which were already well understood in the context of the study, but rather determine the degree and strength of any relationship.

Research Question and Hypotheses

The current study was an exploration of a research question to determine whether correlation existed between the two variables: cultural intelligence and global market orientation. The following research question was asked to provide answers to engineering firm decision makers embarking on business in the global market:

RQ1. What relationship exists between the cultural intelligence and global market orientation of decision makers at U.S.-based engineering organizations entering the global marketplace?

This research question concerned the existence of a correlation between cultural intelligence and global market orientation of decision makers focused on the global marketplace and employed in U.S.-based engineering firms. Creating further definition of the variables, cultural intelligence has four factors that include cognitive, metacognitive, knowledge, and motivational cultural intelligence (Earley & Ang, 2003; Livermore, 2010; Mannor, 2008), while individual market orientation has three factors, namely information acquisition, information sharing, and strategic response (Schlosser, 2004; Schlosser & McNaughton, 2009). Research hypotheses were used to frame the study by addressing potential correlational outcomes.

The research hypotheses set the study's framework by addressing potential outcomes for the data that was collected. The following hypotheses framed this research and highlighted the possible relationships among the variables necessary for the analysis:

H_{O1}: There is no significant relationship between cognitive cultural intelligence and global market information acquisition.

H_{A1}: There is a significant relationship between cognitive cultural intelligence and global market information acquisition.

H_{O2}: There is no significant relationship between metacognitive cultural intelligence and global market information acquisition.

H_{A2}: There is a significant relationship between metacognitive cultural intelligence and global market information acquisition.

H_{O3}: There is no significant relationship between motivational cultural intelligence and global market information acquisition.

H_{A3}: There is a significant relationship between motivational cultural intelligence and global market information acquisition.

H_{O4}: There is no significant relationship between behavioral cultural intelligence and global market information acquisition.

H_{A4}: There is a significant relationship between behavioral cultural intelligence and global market information acquisition.

H_{O5}: There is no significant relationship between cognitive cultural intelligence and global market information sharing.

H_{A5}: There is a significant relationship between cognitive cultural intelligence and global market information sharing.

H_{O6}: There is no significant relationship between metacognitive cultural intelligence and global market information sharing.

H_{A6}: There is a significant relationship between metacognitive cultural intelligence and global market information sharing.

H_{O7}: There is no significant relationship between motivational cultural intelligence and global market information sharing.

H_{A7}: There is a significant relationship between motivational cultural intelligence and global market information sharing.

H_{O8}: There is no significant relationship between behavioral cultural intelligence and global market information sharing.

H_{A8}: There is a significant relationship between behavioral cultural intelligence and global market information sharing.

H_{O9}: There is no significant relationship between cognitive cultural intelligence and global market strategic response.

H_{A9}: There is a significant relationship between cognitive cultural intelligence and global market strategic response.

H_{O10}: There is no significant relationship between metacognitive cultural intelligence and global market strategic response.

H_{A10}: There is a significant relationship between metacognitive cultural intelligence and global market strategic response.

H_{O11}: There is no significant relationship between motivational cultural intelligence and global market strategic response.

H_{A11}: There is a significant relationship between motivational cultural intelligence and global market strategic response.

H_{O12}: There is no significant relationship between behavioral cultural intelligence and global market strategic response.

H_{A12}: There is a significant relationship between behavioral cultural intelligence and global market strategic response.

Population and Geographic Location

The population of this study comprised global decision makers from U.S.-based engineering firms, including Chief Marketing Managers, Chief Executive Officers, Chief Operating Officers, senior marketing managers, and senior business development managers. The total population was extremely large with an estimated 500,000 + decision makers from U.S. engineering firms (American Council of Engineering Companies, 2013). Johnson and Christensen (2012) stated that a study's population is the comprising group that is of prevalent interest and subsequent focus to the researcher. For this study, the population came from U.S.-based engineering design firms that were responsible for senior and corporate-level decision making. The sampling frame consisted of those engineering firms that are ranked by ENR Magazine in 2012 as either a top 150 global design firm or a top 200 international design firm. ENR rankings were based upon a company's 2011 total revenues and total international (non-U.S.) revenues (McGraw-Hill Companies, 2012). ENR ranked international firms based upon non-home country (international) revenue whereas the global design firms were ranked based upon their total global revenue: home country and international (McGraw-Hill Companies, 2012). Though the two lists were separate, many firms appeared on both lists. Discarding any duplicates and non-U.S.-based firms resulted in a total 90 global and/or international design firms. These 90 firms served as the source of the decision makers participating in the study. Based upon a search for U.S.-based firms providing engineering services (NAIC Code: 541330) from the Plunkett Research, Ltd (2013) database, U.S.-based engineering firms have an average of eight company decision makers with the roles adequate for the research. Subsequently, the sampling frame for this study was 720 individuals. Study participants at the top-ranked design firms were located throughout the country in 24 states.

Sampling

Purposive sampling was used for this quantitative correlational study because the sample needed to conform to certain study criteria, namely being global decision makers and working for an engineering firm that was ranked a top-tier global or international firm (Cooper & Schindler, 2003). Neuman (2006) added that researchers use purposive sampling to sample members of a specialized population. For this study, the ENR top firm lists provided the particular foundational data needed for sampling. Purposive sampling was an ideal sampling technique since the study involved a particular field or industry that comprised knowledgeable experts (Tongco, 2007). The global engineering field encompasses decision makers with particular global marketplace knowledge and information who were critical to answering the study's research question. Tongco (2007) and Johnson and Christensen (2012) indicated that purposive sampling is commonly used in both quantitative and qualitative research studies.

Lund Research Ltd (2013) suggested that researcher judgment plays a significant role in purposive sampling particularly when selecting the individuals, organizations, and data to be studied. Leader contact data of top-ranked global/international design firms were accessed from ENR's Global Sourcebook ranked listings, which were publicly available on ENR's website, and by searching each individual company's website. Additional firm contact data of global decision makers, including email addresses, were collected through public agency procurement listings, public libraries, annual reports, and through personal contacts. Although purposive sampling was a logical selection for this study, the sampling technique had weaknesses. One weakness was that purposive sampling relies upon a participant's reliability (Tongco, 2007). Suppressing this inherent weakness, the study involved participants who were senior decision makers at reliable global or international design firms that were corroborated by ENR magazine. Another weakness of purposive sampling was that the sample being studied may not have been representative of the population (Lund Research Ltd, 2013; Neuman, 2006). This weakness was significantly diminished by using credible and acknowledged global leaders whose knowledge of and actions in the global marketplace were measurable particularly by global or international revenues. These U.S. leaders' insights into the global engineering market may be generalizable to the population of U.S. engineering firm leaders embracing the global market.

The sample consisted of participants who were characterized as senior decision makers at U.S.-based engineering firms listed by ENR magazine as one of the top global design and/or international design firms designated by the design firm's 2011 revenues. The sample included a mix of Chief Marketing Managers, Chief Executive Officers, Chief Operating Officers, senior marketing managers, and senior business development managers. The sample sufficiently represented the entire population because similar company decision makers who face similar global market decisions were present in domestic engineering companies doing business globally.

Gay, Mills, and Airasian (2011) stated that at least 30 participants are necessary to conduct a correlational study. Based on the total sampling frame of 720 with a confidence level of 95% and a confidence interval of 6.5, the target sample size was 227 global design decision makers (MaCorr Research, 2013). An initial 600 individuals were randomly chosen to participate in the study based on the individual's availability to complete the survey. Each individual in the sampling frame was alphabetized by last name in Microsoft Excel and assigned a unique, sequential number (1 to 720). Selection of the participants was accomplished using the random generator website *Randomizer.org*. The expected response rate was 38% of the purposive sample or approximately 228 decision makers. This expected response rate was compliant with Church and Waclawski's (2001) distinction that typical response rates in organizations range between 30 and 85 percent. Depending on the actual amount of valid responses and to account for invalid and non-responses, randomly selected replacements were chosen until the number of acceptable returns equaled or exceeded the necessary sample size of 384 individuals. Selection of the replacement participants was accomplished using the random generator website (*Randomizer.org*) and the original sequentially numbered, alphabetized list of potential participants. Unfortunately, the response rate for the study was lower than expected with 38 decision makers successfully responding. Although the sample size was small, the study met reliable correlational study requirements (Gay, Mills, & Airasian, 2011), and was therefore credible and generalizable to the population.

Informed Consent, Confidentiality, and Data Retention

Participant informed awareness, privacy, and confidentiality was vital to this study. Cooper and Schindler (2003) stated that participant informed consent involved disclosing the study's purpose along with the methods and processes that were undertaken during the study prior to proceeding with the survey. The informed consent form outlined the study's purpose, process, voluntary participation, and anticipated timeframe for completion. Participants were assured that their responses were confidential and anonymous, with individual responses not appearing in the research findings. Each participant received a link to the informed consent form website and was required to read the informed consent form with the choice to either agree and join the study or decline participation and close the website. Participants were required to download, read, print, physically sign, and return an informed consent form (Appendix A) hosted on *GoogleDrive* website prior to obtaining the secure survey website link and starting the surveys. Through agreement, signature and return of the informed consent, the participant confirmed that he/she was the person invited to take the surveys and was the participant to take the surveys. Return of the signed form was completed in one of three ways: 1) faxing the signed form to (207) 293-4693; 2) emailing a scan of the signed form to *sgalati1026@email.phoenix.edu*; or 3) mailing the signed form to: Galati-Consent Form, 14 Gabriel Drive, Augusta, Maine 04330. If the informed consent form was declined, the participant's invitation was withdrawn and the participant was not given the link to the surveys.

Once the signed informed consent form was received, the participant was emailed a link to a separate, confidential survey website hosted by *SurveyMonkey*. Both surveys and the demographic questions resided on the same *SurveyMonkey* website, but completely separate from the Informed Consent *GoogleDrive* website. Appendix B contains a copy of the permission to use *SurveyMonkey* as the study's survey tool. Upon completion of the first survey, the participant was automatically sent to the second survey and demographic questions.

As part of the demographic questions, participants were asked to enter their assigned research PIN number comprised of six alphanumeric digits. Each participant research PIN was unique, created using the alphanumeric string generator from *Sweepjudge.com*, and was assigned during participant engagement (discussed later in the data collection section). The individual participant and the researcher were the only persons to know the assigned PIN number to ensure confidentiality. If the participant wished to withdraw after submitting the survey responses, the participant had to email a withdraw request to *sgalati1026@email.phoenix.edu* disclosing the PIN number. The PIN helped identify which survey pack to discard. If by chance the withdrawing participant forgot the PIN, the researcher could have looked-up the assigned research PIN and withdrawn the survey responses. Withdrawing from the study could happen at any time.

Through the informed consent form, participants were assured of confidentiality. The form specified that: (a) the participant's identity would remain confidential and the participant's name would not be made known to any outside party; (b) there were no foreseeable risks associated with participation; (c) participants could withdraw from the study at any time without problem or any loss of benefits and privacy; (d) participants received specific instructions and contact information if they decide to withdraw; and (e) the responses were securely retained and destroyed. All data is being retained for five years from the completion date of the study and subsequently destroyed. During storage, all electronic data is stored on a dedicated external hard drive and password protected using a high security password of more than six characters incorporating at least one capital letter, one lowercase letter, an alphanumeric character, and a number. All hardcopy data is being kept in a secure and locked area in Mount Vernon, Maine. Data purging and destruction of all data will involve reformatting the dedicated hard drive and using cross-hatched shredding for all hardcopies. Data retention and destruction will be astutely handled by only the researcher.

Instrumentation

In the study, two different survey instruments were employed: the CQS (Ang et al., 2007; Van Dyne, Ang, & Koh, 2009) and the I-MARKOR (Schlosser & McNaughton, 2009). The CQS (Ang et al., 2007; Van Dyne, Ang, & Koh, 2009) was used to assess participant cultural intelligence and assess the participant's levels of motivational, behavioral, cognitive, and metacognitive cultural intelligence. The I-MARKOR (Schlosser & McNaughton, 2009) was used to evaluate global market orientation on the individual level and assess the participant's levels of information acquisition, information sharing, and strategic response levels. Demographic data was collected as part of the study and was used for demographic statistical analysis. Participants were provided answers to questions on gender, age, geographic location, role in their organization, years of experience in their organization, and years of experience in the global marketplace. Appendix C contains permission to use the surveys, Appendix D contains copies of each survey, and Appendix E contains a copy of the demographic questions used with the surveys.

Cultural Intelligence Scale

The Cultural Intelligence Scale (CQS) is a 20-item scale used for the self-assessment and peer-assessment of cultural intelligence levels, both on a cumulative level and on an individual factor level (Van Dyne, Ang, & Koh, 2009). The scale consists of four sections (one for each cultural intelligence component): (a) CQ-Strategy; (b) CQ-Knowledge; (c) CQ-Motivation; and (d) CQ-Behavior. The instrument's CQ-Strategy questions represent the metacognitive component of cultural intelligence, while the CQ-Knowledge questions represent the cognitive component of cultural intelligence (Ang et al., 2007; Cultural Intelligence Center, 2005). The CQ-Motivation and CQ-Behavior questions on the CQS represent their namesake components of cultural intelligence: motivational and behavioral respectively (Ang et al., 2007; Cultural Intelligence Center, 2005). The scale items have strong psychometric properties, comprising four items for metacognitive measurement, six items for cognitive measurement, five items for motivational measurement, and five items for behavioral measurement (Ang et al., 2007; Van Dyne, Ang, & Koh, 2009). A seven-ranking Likert scale was used, ranging from 1 (*strongly disagree*) to 7 (*strongly agree*), to assess individual cultural intelligence from the perspective of the participant's personal experience.

The CQS is a validated and reliable instrument. Ang, et al. (2007) examined the scale's psychometric properties and provided cross-validation analysis of the scale. This analysis offered strong empirical support for the validity, stability, and reliability of the scale, and reinforced its generalization across time and geographic locations. Ang et al. (2007) also concluded that the four components of cultural intelligence have differential relationships with explicit intercultural effectiveness outcomes, including cognitive, affective, and behavioral outcomes. This means that each of the four components of cultural intelligence have a specific influence on outcome. This first cross-validation effort suggested that the CQS could be used with a high level confidence (Ang et al., 2007; Van Dyne, Ang, & Koh, 2009).

Van Dyne, Ang, and Koh (2009) continued the validation work of Ang et al. (2007) and provided substantial construct validity of the scale. They stated that the rigorous CQS development process provided a vibrant four-factor structure and reinforced the Ang et al. (2007) analysis that the CQS is stable across samples, time, countries, and cultures. As part of the scale development, Ang et al. (2007) conducted confirmatory factor analysis to examine the stability of the four factor structure. They found that the four factor model fit the data better than a three factor, two factor, or one factor model through the Comparative Fit Indices of 0.92, 0.88, 0.81, and 0.75 respectively. Through confirmatory analysis, they found that the CQS has a high internal consistency and test-retest reliability for each component of cultural intelligence. Composite reliability analysis showed strong factor dimension reliability with Cronbach's alpha (α)=0.71 for metacognitive cultural intelligence, α=0.85 for cognitive cultural intelligence, α=0.75 for motivational cultural intelligence, and α=0.83 for behavioral (Ang et al., 2007; VanDyne, Ang, & Koh, 2008). Van Dyne, Ang, and Koh (2009) indicated that composite reliabilities exceeded the α=0.70 threshold and concluded that the CQS is a reliable and valid measure of cultural intelligence.

I-MARKOR Scale

The I-MARKOR (Schlosser & McNaughton, 2009) is a 20-item scale used for the assessment of individual market orientation. The scale consists of statements representing three areas: (a) information acquisition; (b) information sharing; and (c) strategic response (Ho, Niden, & Johneny, 2011; Schlosser, 2004; Schlosser & McNaughton, 2009). The scale items had strong psychometric properties, comprising eight items for information acquisition, seven items for information sharing, and five items for strategic response (Ho, Niden, & Johneny, 2011). A five-ranking Likert scale was used on the I-MARKOR, ranging from 1 (*never*) to 5 (*almost always*), to assess individual market orientation from the perspective of the participant's personal actions and understandings. All 20 statements required two responses: one response for whether the participant felt obligated to do the stated action (under *I should*) and one response for whether the participant actually did the stated action (under *I do*). The first response to questions (*I should*) represented the participant's market orientation action understanding whereas the second response (*I do*) represented market orientation implementation. According to Schlosser (2004), the dual responses per item are important and were added to the final scale to help make the I-MARKOR generalizable outside the financial industry. References to the terms *customer* and *distributor* were clarified to help better generalize the scale as well (Schlosser, 2004).

The I-MARKOR was deemed valid and reliable by Schlosser and McNaughton (2009), which was further supported by Ho, Niden, and Joheneny (2011). Validation of the I-MARKOR scale involved construct reliability analysis, examination of convergent and discriminant validity, and nomological validity. Schlosser and McNaughton (2009) developed the I-MARKOR from initially 71 potential measurable items gathered from the behaviors discussed among focus groups. After three iterations of purification pre-testing, namely with industry practitioners (pretests #1 and #3) and academic researchers (pretest #2), the I-MARKOR evolved into a 20-item scale (Schlosser & McNaughton, 2009).

Confirmatory factor analysis was conducted on the 20-item scale to examine the stability of the factor structures. Schlosser and McNaughton (2009) found that the three-factor model fit the data better than a two-factor model or a single (first-order) factor model through the Comparative Fit Indices of 0.926, 0.862, and 0.792 respectively. Construct reliability analysis showed overall high scale reliability with a Cronbach's alpha (α) of 0.9409 and high factor dimensions scale reliabilities of $\alpha=0.9250$ for information acquisition, $\alpha=0.8864$ for information sharing, and $\alpha=0.8370$ for strategic response (Schlosser & McNaughton, 2009). The stability and construct reliability analysis confirmed that the three-factor structure holds an appropriate data fit with how employees acquire, share, and respond to market information.

Originally, the scale was developed for a financial services organization; however, the scale was found to measure good work practices that are translatable to many roles and found to be implementable by different people in different ways. Ho, Niden, and Joheneny (2011) used a slightly modified I-MARKOR for stockbroking firms in Malaysia. Schlosser and McNaughton (2009) substantiated the scale to be a measure of dynamic capability.

Data Collection

Prior to receiving the consent form, the sampling of global decision makers received a personalized email (see Appendix F) that detailed the study parameters, described the logistical aspects to the study, assigned a unique participant research PIN, and invited them to join the study. The research PIN was created using the alphanumeric string generator from *Sweepjudge.com*. The link to the online informed consent form was included. As incentive, the email stated that copies of the findings will be made available to the participants for their information and use.

The research data for the study was collected through *SurveyMonkey*, a flexible online survey tool, and was include the following data items: (a) demographic questions, such as gender, age, geographic location, role in their organization, years of experience in their organization, and years of experience in the global marketplace; (b) the CQS survey; and (c) the I-MARKOR survey. Participants had to acknowledge, sign, and return the online informed consent form prior to receiving the survey website link. Participants were requested to complete the surveys within five working days.

The online format of the survey was used to offer convenience and response flexibility (for example, participants can respond using a laptop, ipad, iPhone, or any Wi-Fi-compatible device), accommodate different geographic areas of the participants, ensure confidentiality, and promote time flexibility. The online survey had a designated time to remain active; however, every effort was made to ensure an adequate sample size. Survey questions were presented to the participants in the same order. Once completed, participants were thanked for their input and reminded of confidentiality.

Threats to Validity and Reliability

The current study was intended for applied science and real world use, and was dependent upon a valid and reliable research approach. Johnson and Christensen (2012) concurred that research validity infers truthfulness in the study findings. However, research validity and reliability can be compromised by threats inherent in the study's design. Threats to research validity involve design concerns that jeopardize the accuracy and reliability of the research findings and analysis (Salkind, 2003). Ultimately, threats can imperil both internal and external validity.

The study may also be considered reliable and consistent across other populations and study settings. Salkind (2003) and Neuman (2006) stated that a representative research reliability advocates a repeatability and consistency of the results across different populations. This study's research reliability was essential to engage future research study of the variables. Understanding the threats to the study and the controls used to mitigate these threats may have provided assurance for the accuracy of the findings and may provide future studies with a stable research foundation. Following are discussions about threats to the study's internal and external validity, as well as how these validation threats were minimized or eliminated.

Internal Validity

First introduced by Campbell and Stanley (1963) and refined by Cook and Campbell (1979), internal validity is "the ability to infer that a casual relationship exists between two variables" (Johnson & Christensen, 2012, p. 247). The objective of this study was to identify valid inferences about the correlations between the two variables: cultural intelligence and global market orientation. Conducting valid research, data analysis, and conclusions necessitate the reduction or elimination of any threats to internal validity. Potential internal validity threats to research studies include maturation, namely psychological or biological changes; selection; testing; instrumentation, regression, and mortality. Behi and Nolan (1996) suggested that other threats may include compensatory rivalry among participants, the selection of participants, and history when time passes from when the study begins and ends. Although there are numerous potential threats for research, the specific threats to this study included instrumentation and compensatory rivalry threats.

Instrumentation posed threats, however minimal, to this study through the global context imposed on the I-MARKOR survey. Traditionally, the I-MARKOR has been used for a geographically distinct marketplace; however, this study imposed a context that covers all geographies in the world and was geographically non-distinct. Even though the measurement of the I-MARKOR was the same, the broadening of context may have imposed a nominal threat.

Minimizing the internal validity threats from instrumentation was accomplished through the use of validated and reliable instruments, namely the CQS and I-MARKOR. Although the context imposed on the I-MARKOR scale was global, the type of marketplace was distinct (engineering) and the sampled population was limited to a single geographic location: the United States. By focusing the study and use of the instrument on a specific service type and geographic populous, the threats imposed on the study from instrumentation were mitigated. According to Onwuegbuzie (2000), instrumentation threats cannot be eliminated fully since any outcome measurement cannot be flawless.

Compensatory rivalry threats occur to internal validity when public knowledge of the study causes individual or participant groups to feel like an underdog or somehow inferior to other participants (Behi & Nolan, 1996). Although not completely akin to this study, compensatory rivalry threats could have occurred to some degree on this study if participants recognized that their competitors were invited to complete the surveys too. Embellishment of experience and knowledge could creep into the participant responses as a mechanism against appearing inferior to competition on any level.

The compensatory rivalry threats to the study were minimized through the control of public information disclosure. The fact that all participants worked for ENR-ranked top design firms was not disclosed in the written materials describing the study. By controlling the disclosure of information to the public, participants had no source for legitimizing their suspicions about fellow participants and competitor participation in the research study. Participants were less likely to embellish or overstate their individual global experience. Similar to internal validity, threats also existed for the study's external validity.

External Validity

External validity, also first introduced by Campbell and Stanley (1963) and expanded by Cook and Campbell (1979), involves the degree to which the study's findings and outcomes can be generalized across populations, time, situations, and differential treatments (Cooper & Schindler, 2003). External validity was important to this study. A lack of external validity will make the findings true only for research purposes, but useless in real world applications and applied sciences (Neuman, 2006). Johnson and Christensen (2012) stated that sampling populations of individuals, environments, timeframes, and outcomes are rarely done because of the time and cost commitment for the researcher. Consequently, all studies have elements that threaten external validity (Johnson & Christensen, 2012).

Threats to external validity related to the generalizability of the study. For this study, the population selection posed threats to external validity. Cooper and Schindler (2003) stated that researchers typically draw samples from accessible populations rather than a preferred random sampling from a large population. For this study, the sample frame encompassed an accessible and well-documented selection of senior decision makers from top domestic engineering firms. The study's sample frame comprised a smaller defined group of decision makers from global firms that resulted in a diminished generalizability to that of a study with a very large and less defined participant pool.

The sample frame consisted of documented leaders in the global marketplace to control the threats from population selection. These individuals were from leading engineering companies that by the nature of the industry had relevance and relatedness to other, less experienced, but global bound, engineering firms. Kinship to other less experienced firms was evident by the fact that the top four global engineering design firms made up less than 10 percent of the industry market share (IBISWorld Inc., 2012). This relatedness added credence to the generalizability of the sample and, consequently mitigated any population selection threats to external validity. Demographic information was also collected from participants during the study to provide information on any unintended sampling bias that was present and could affect the results. Identifying a sampling bias impeded the generalizability of the sample.

Data Analysis

Data collected by participants through the online survey was analyzed using descriptive and correlational statistic methods. Descriptive statistical analysis was conducted on demographic data, and included mean, median, mode, and standard deviation calculations. Data collected from the surveys was entered in SPSS, a software application used for statistical analysis and prediction in the social sciences. Microsoft Excel was also used for the descriptive statistical calculations.

The Spearman's rho (ρ) correlation coefficient was used in this study because it measures the significance of relationships between variable data (Triola, 2005). This collected data was measured on an ordinal level.

According to Randolph and Myers (2013) and Cooper and Schindler (2003), the Spearman's rho (ρ) coefficient, which is an alternative to the parametric Pearson's product-moment correlation coefficient, must be used on ordinal-level data. The Spearman's rho (ρ) coefficient measured the degree of association between cultural intelligence and market orientation. Data analysis was used to determine the presence of a positive or negative correlation. The coefficient always is a value between -1.00 and +1.00. If the calculated value of the correlation coefficient was close to or equal to zero, then it was interpreted as no significant linear correlation (weak association) between the variables. Alternately, if the calculated value of the correlation coefficient was close to -1.00 or +1.00, then it was interpreted as having a significant linear correlation (or strong association) between the variables (Triola, 2005). Coefficient values close to -1.00 indicated a negative correlation, while values close to +1.00 indicated a positive correlation. Negative correlations meant that values for each variable move in opposite directions (when x increases, y decreases), whereas positive correlations meant that values for each variable move was the same direction (when x increases, y increases) (Randolph & Myers, 2013). If a correlation was found to exist (a positive correlation of at least +0.70 or a negative correlation of at least -0.70), linear regression analysis was used to further understand the correlation and the best linear relationship between data.

Summary

The quantitative method and correlational non-experimental explanatory study design were discussed as an appropriate method and design for this study. A quantitative research method was chosen to understand the relationships between cultural intelligence and market orientation within domestic engineering firms aimed at the global marketplace. This study's primary focus was to recognize any influences or relationships the two variables, cultural intelligence and market orientation, have on each other. The qualitative method was not suitable for the research because it did not involve the measurements needed for determining variable relationships.

This study's population included 720 global decision makers from top-ranked U.S.-based engineering design firms. These decision makers included individuals in such roles as Chief Marketing Managers, Chief Executive Officers, Chief Operating Officers, senior marketing managers, and senior business development managers. Purposive sampling was used for this quantitative correlational study because the population, based on ENR magazine's 2012 rankings, was experts within the global engineering field. A weakness of purposive sampling was dependence on participant reliability; however, the sample consisted of decision makers from credible, ENR-corroborated global design firms located in the U.S. Although another weakness was that the sample may not be representative of the population, the sample was comprised of acknowledged global leaders who have measurable outcomes. The target sample size was 227 global design decision makers; however that target was not met in the study.

Participants had to acknowledge, sign, and return an informed consent form prior to beginning the surveys. Informed consent assured participant confidentiality and specified guidelines for participant withdrawal from the study, and response data retention and destruction. Participants provided demographic data as part of the study, including answers to questions on gender, age, geographic location, role and years of experience in the organization, and years of experience in the global marketplace. All data will be retained for five years and subsequently destroyed.

The chapter covered the validity, reliability, and use of two different survey instruments: the CQS (Ang et al., 2007; Van Dyne, Ang, & Koh, 2009) and the I-MARKOR (Schlosser & McNaughton, 2009). Both survey instruments were formally validated as reliable survey measurement tools. The CQS is a 20-item scale used for the self-assessment and peer-assessment of cultural intelligence levels, and consists of four sections: (a) CQ-Strategy; (b) CQ-Knowledge; (c) CQ-Motivation; and (d) CQ-Behavior (Van Dyne, Ang, & Koh, 2009). The I-MARKOR is a 20-item scale used for the assessment of individual market orientation that represents three areas: (a) information acquisition; (b) information sharing; and (c) strategic response (Ho, Niden, & Johneny, 2011; Schlosser, 2004; Schlosser & McNaughton, 2009).

SurveyMonkey, an online survey tool, was used for the research data collection. Participants were requested to complete the survey within five working days. The survey tool was selected because it promotes flexibility for the participant to respond. The research reliability and validity were discussed in detail, particularly how the researcher minimized or eliminated internal and external validity threats. Such threats included internal threats, such as participant selection, testing, and instrumentation, and external threats, such as multiple treatments, experimenter effects, and pretest sensitization. The data analysis approach was also discussed, including use of descriptive statistical analysis, Spearman's rho (ρ) correlation calculation, and linear regression for any positive correlations. Data analysis and computations were completed using SPSS software and Microsoft Excel as statistical analytic tools. In Chapter 4, the findings of the research are presented and discussed centering on the statistical analyses of the collected study data. Findings included all hypotheses test results as well as other research findings from the collected demographic data.

FOUR

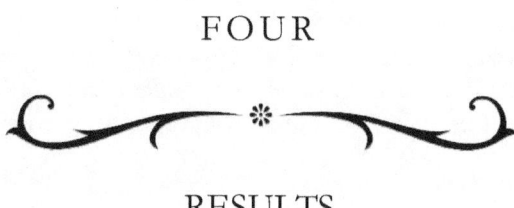

RESULTS

The purpose of this quantitative correlational study was to determine any relationship between the independent variables of cultural intelligence and market orientation of decision makers at U.S.-based engineering firms to the dependent variable of entering the global marketplace. In addressing the study's purpose, the researcher studied the following research question: What relationship exists between the cultural intelligence and global market orientation of decision makers at U.S.-based engineering organizations entering the global marketplace?

Data was collected from participating respondents (N=38) using two validated survey instruments and targeted demographic questions through the survey website, *surveymonkey.com*. Respondents were invited through email with a link to the Informed Consent. Once the signed and returned Informed Consent was received, the participating individual received a link to the survey. All respondents completed the online demographic questions along with online versions of the Cultural Intelligence Scale (Ang et al., 2007; Van Dyne, Ang, & Koh, 2009) and I-MARKOR (Schlosser, 2004; Schlosser & McNaughton, 2009) instruments. All respondents completed the demographic and instrument questions sequentially within the same survey website.

Chapter 4 includes the descriptive and statistical analyses of the collected data. Presented in four sections, the results of this study follow. Presented in the first section are demographic data and analysis of the responses. The second section comprises the hypotheses test results. The third section contains analysis of the relationship between Cultural Intelligence and Global Market Orientation through examination of each cumulative score. The fourth section comprises a summary of the key findings based upon the data results.

Demographic Analysis

The survey facilitated collection of demographic data about the respondents. This data described the respondent's gender, age, ethnicity, race, length in the current role, length with the current company, and the types of engineering marketed globally. Microsoft Excel and IBM's SPSS Statistics Version 21 software facilitated the statistical analysis.

Gender of Respondents

Table 2 indicates that more males responded to the survey than females by nearly two thirds to one third. All respondents specified gender. Male respondents comprised 65.79% and female respondents comprised 34.21%.

Table 2
The gender of respondents (N=38).

Category	Frequency	Percentage
Male	25	65.79%
Female	13	34.21%

Age of Respondents

Table 3 indicates that nearly half of the respondents were between 51 and 60 years of age. Nearly a quarter of the respondents were over 80 years of age. The remaining individuals, all within the *21-30, 41-50,* and *71-80* age groups, comprised a little more than a quarter of the respondents cumulatively, were disseminated. The respondents included none under 21 years of age or within the ages of 31-40 and 61-70.

Table 3
The age of respondents (N=38).

Category	Frequency	Percentage
Under 21	0	0%
21 - 30	7	18.42%
31 - 40	0	0%
41 - 50	2	5.26%
51 - 60	18	47.37%
61 - 70	0	0%
71 - 80	2	5.26%
Over 80	9	23.68%

Ethnic Background

Nearly all of the study respondents, specifically 97.37%, were of Non-Hispanic / Latino ethnicity. The remaining 2.63% of the respondents were of Hispanic / Latino ethnicity. Table 4 indicates the frequency and percentage breakdowns for the ethnicity of the respondents.

Table 4
The ethnicity of respondents (N=38).

Category	Frequency	Percentage
Hispanic / Latino	1	2.63%
Non-Hispanic / Latino	37	97.37%

Race of Respondents

Table 5 indicates the distribution of races among respondents. More than four-fifths of the respondents were of White / Caucasian / European descent. The races of the remaining respondents, which made up less than one fifth of all respondents, were Black / African (2.63%), South Asian (5.26%), East Asian (2.63%), and Native American (2.63%). There were no respondents with Middle Eastern, Pacific Islander, or other origins.

Table 5
Race of respondents (N=38).

Category	Frequency	Percentage
White / Caucasian / European	33	86.84%
Black / African	1	2.63%
South Asian (Indian Subcontinent)	2	5.26%
East Asian (China, Korea, Japan, Thailand, etc.)	1	2.63%
Native American	1	2.63%
Middle Eastern	0	0%
Pacific Islander	0	0%
Other	0	0%

Length in Current Role

Table 6 indicates the respondents' length in their current role with their company. The majority of the respondents (31.58%) were in their current role between 6-10 years. The responses were distributed closely between the current role length categories of 3-5 years (18.42%) and more than 20 years (21.05%). The three length in current role categories accounted for nearly three quarters of the respondents at 71.05%. The remaining three categories were the 11-15 years (13.16%), 16-20 years (10.53%), and 1-2 years (5.26%). There were no respondents in their role less than one year.

Table 6
Respondents' length in current role (N=38).

Category	Frequency	Percentage
Less than 1 year	0	0%
1 – 2 years	2	5.26%
3 – 5 years	7	18.42%
6 – 10 years	12	31.58%
11 – 15 years	5	13.16%
16 – 20 years	4	10.53%
More than 20 years	8	21.05%

Length with Current Company

Table 7 indicates the respondents' tenure with their current company. Responses to length (tenure) with the current company had more uniform distribution through all of the categories. The 6-10 years length comprised the largest concentration of respondents with 26.32% of all respondents. Responses were nearly equally distributed between the 1-2 years, 3-5 years, 11-15 years, and more than 20 years categories with 15.79%, 10.53%, 15.79%, and 21.05% respectively. The categories of less than 1 year (5.26%) and 16- 20 years (5.26%) were equal and completed the distribution.

Table 7
Respondents' length with current company (N=38).

Category	Frequency	Percentage
Less than 1 year	2	5.26%
1 – 2 years	6	15.79%
3 – 5 years	4	10.53%
6 – 10 years	10	26.32%
11 – 15 years	6	15.79%
16 – 20 years	2	5.26%
More than 20 years	8	21.05%

Types of Engineering Marketed Globally

Table 8 indicates the types of engineering services marketed globally by respondents. More than half of the respondents reported that they market environmental, power, and civil engineering with 71.05%, 60.53%, and 55.26% respectively. These three engineering services, marking the third and fourth quartiles of responses, make up the highest concentration of respondent-marketed areas. The second quartile of respondents indicated the global marketing of transportation (50.00%), green/sustainability (47.37%), structural (47.37%), electrical (44.74%), mechanical (31.58%), and geotechnical (26.32%) engineering services. Incidentally, this second quartile grouping marks the second highest concentration of respondents. Less than a quarter of the respondents (first quartile) reported marketing the remaining 15 selected engineering services, as specifically detailed on Table 8. No respondents reported the remaining three engineering services: marketing aerospace, biomolecular, or nanoengineering.

Table 8
The types of engineering marketed globally by respondents (N=38).

Category	Frequency	Percentage
Acoustical	1	2.63%
Aerospace	0	0%
Agricultural	1	2.63%
Biomedical	1	2.63%
Biomolecular	0	0%
Chemical	7	18.42%
Civil	21	55.26%
Computer/Software	2	5.26%
Electrical	17	44.74%
Environmental	27	71.05%
Geotechnical	10	26.32%
Green / Sustainability	18	47.37%
Industrial	7	18.42%
Manufacturing	2	5.26%
Materials	2	5.26%
Mechanical	12	31.58%
Minerals / Mining	5	13.16%
Nanoengineering	0	0%
Nuclear	9	23.68%
Oceanic	1	2.63%
Petroleum	5	13.16%
Power	23	60.53%
Process	5	13.16%
Seismic	8	21.05%
Structural	18	47.37%
Traffic	8	21.05%
Transportation	19	50.00%

Instruments

The research survey involved the demographic data discussed in the previous section and two validated instruments: the Cultural Intelligence Scale (CQS) and the I-MARKOR Individual Market Orientation scale. The I-MARKOR (Schlosser, 2004; Schlosser & McNaughton, 2009) provided the measurement for individual market orientation including the three focus areas: Information Acquisition, Information Sharing, and Strategic Response. The CQS (Ang et al., 2007; Van Dyne, Ang, & Koh, 2009) provided the instrument to measure the independent variable of cultural intelligence including the four focus areas" motivational CQ, Behavioral CQ, Cognitive CQ, and Metacognitive CQ. The following subsections provide descriptive statistical analysis of each instrument conducted using Microsoft Excel and IBM's SPSS Statistics Version 21 software.

I-MARKOR Individual Market Orientation Scale

Table 9 presents the descriptive statistics for each of the I-MARKOR questions. The I-MARKOR survey instrument appears in Appendix D. A five-ranking Likert scale was used on the I-MARKOR, ranging from 1 (*never*) to 5 (*almost always*), to assess individual market orientation from the perspective of the participant's personal actions and understandings. All 20 statements require two responses: one response for whether the participant feels obligated to do the stated action (under *I should*) and one response for whether the participant actually does the stated action (under *I do*). The I-MARKOR questions have strong psychometric properties, comprising eight questions for information acquisition, seven questions for information sharing, and five questions for strategic response (Ho, Niden, & Johneny, 2011).

The survey question receiving the highest mean score for strongest (positive) agreement, 4.50, was question 23: *I should/I do take action when I find out that customers are unhappy with the quality of our service.* The survey questions with the lowest mean scores were questions 10 and 25 (both with a score of 3.01) and question 20. Question 10 stated: *I should/I do ask distributors to assess the quality of our products and services.* Question 20 stated: *I should/I do review our product development efforts with distributors to ensure that they are in line with what customers want.* Question 25 stated: *I should/I do try to help distributors achieve their goals.* Question 23, which had the highest mean score, also had the second lowest standard deviation (0.71) tied with question 16: *I should/I do participate in interdepartmental meetings to discuss market trends and developments.* The lowest standard deviation of responses was 0.63 for question 22: *I should/I do coordinate my activities with the activities of coworkers or departments in this organization.* The overall mean of the I-MARKOR survey sample was 3.66 over a 5-point scale with a standard deviation of 1.01.

Table 9 included coefficients that indicated positive distribution skewing in some I-MARKOR responses. Discernable skewness exists if the absolute value of the skewness coefficient is less than two times the associated standard error. Questions 12, 13, and 23 had the most significant distribution skewness from the I-MARKOR questions. Questions 12 and 13 also had the largest Kurtosis coefficients, which indicated sharp distribution peaks. Questions 12 and 13 invited information acquisition factor responses, whereas question 23 invited strategic response factor responses.

Table 9
I-MARKOR Scale Descriptive Statistics

Question	Min.	Max.	Mean	Std. Dev.	Skewness*	Kurtosis**
9	1	5	3.58	1.23	-0.794	-0.199
10	1	5	3.01	1.14	-0.531	-0.399
11	1	5	3.20	1.09	-0.602	-0.088
12	1	5	3.86	0.98	-1.395	2.264
13	1	5	3.78	1.00	-1.305	1.880
14	1	5	3.22	1.12	-0.446	-0.319
15	1	5	3.54	0.87	-0.789	1.026
16	2.5	5	3.89	0.71	-0.027	-0.849
17	1	5	3.47	1.01	-0.954	0.986
18	1.5	5	4.13	0.84	-0.918	0.916
19	1	5	3.71	1.00	-0.955	1.188
20	1	5	3.03	1.12	-0.419	-0.099
21	1	5	3.92	1.02	-1.012	0.630
22	3	5	4.28	0.63	-0.419	-0.735
23	2.5	5	4.50	0.71	-1.271	0.666
24	2	5	3.80	0.90	-0.196	-0.908
25	1	5	3.01	1.29	-0.131	-1.006
26	1	5	3.79	1.22	-0.973	0.132
27	1	5	3.95	1.26	-1.008	0.182
28	1	5	3.58	1.08	-1.094	0.868
Total			3.66	1.01	-0.762	0.307

* Skewness Standard Error = 0.383
** Kurtosis Standard Error = 0.750

Tables 10 – 12 include analysis for each of the I-MARKOR questions demarcated by *I should* and *I do* responses. The segregation of these I-MARKOR response tables are by market orientation factor, namely Information Acquisition, Information Sharing, and Strategic Response.

Table 10
Information Acquisition Factor: I-MARKOR Scale Question Response Analysis

Question	1. Never	2. Almost Never	3. Sometimes	4. Often	5. Almost Always
9: I should	4	3	5	14	12
9: I do	4	3	11	12	8
10: I should	6	3	12	11	6
10: I do	7	3	20	6	2
11: I should	4	3	10	13	8
11: I do	6	5	16	8	3
12: I should	2	1	4	18	13
12: I do	2	3	6	21	6
13: I should	2	1	5	19	11
13: I do	3	2	9	17	7
14: I should	4	2	12	12	8
14: I do	5	10	8	11	4
15: I should	1	3	9	16	9
15: I do	1	4	18	12	3
20: I should	6	1	12	13	6
20: I do	7	5	20	3	3

Table 11
Information Sharing Factor: I-MARKOR Scale Question Response Analysis

Question	1. Never	2. Almost Never	3. Sometimes	4. Often	5. Almost Always
16: I should	0	0	9	14	15
16: I do	0	3	14	15	6
17: I should	3	1	7	18	9
17: I do	3	6	13	13	3
18: I should	0	1	6	12	19
18: I do	1	0	11	13	13
19: I should	2	1	5	19	11
19: I do	3	4	10	14	7
21: I should	1	3	3	13	18
21: I do	1	5	10	11	11
22: I should	0	0	3	15	20
22: I do	0	0	9	16	13
24: I should	0	2	10	14	12
24: I do	0	5	12	12	9

Table 12
Strategic Response Factor: I-MARKOR Scale Question Response Analysis

Question	1. Never	2. Almost Never	3. Sometimes	4. Often	5. Almost Always
23: I should	0	0	3	5	30
23: I do	0	2	7	7	22
25: I should	6	5	10	10	7
25: I do	8	6	13	6	5
26: I should	3	2	6	11	16
26: I do	3	4	7	13	11
27: I should	3	1	8	5	21
27: I do	3	1	13	3	18
28: I should	3	1	8	15	11
28: I do	4	3	10	17	4

The boxplot chart for the I-MARKOR scale data (see Figure 2) was developed to further understand the distribution and data values. Boxplot charts are used to graphically detect deviations from normal distribution, including assumption violations, skewness, and data outliers (Randolph & Myers, 2013). As is evident in Figure 2, the boxplot showed symmetrical distribution for information acquisition factor, slight left skewed distribution (higher values) for the information sharing factor, and slight right skewed distribution (lower values) for the strategic response factor. The chart clarified the skewness values in Table 9 and provided graphical representation that the distribution skewness was minor.

Based on Figure 2, the information acquisition factor had a range of 42 and interquartile range of 12. The information sharing factor had a range of 37 and interquartile range of 12. The strategic response factor had a range of 28 and an interquartile range of 8. Additionally, the strategic response factor had a significantly lower score than the other two market orientation factors. Additionally, Figure 2 revealed outliers (Cases 20, 24, and 36) for information acquisition and strategic response (only cases 20 and 24), which indicated the values are abnormal. Because these outlier cases had relevant outcomes for other market orientation factors, Case 20, 24, and 36 were retained in the research study.

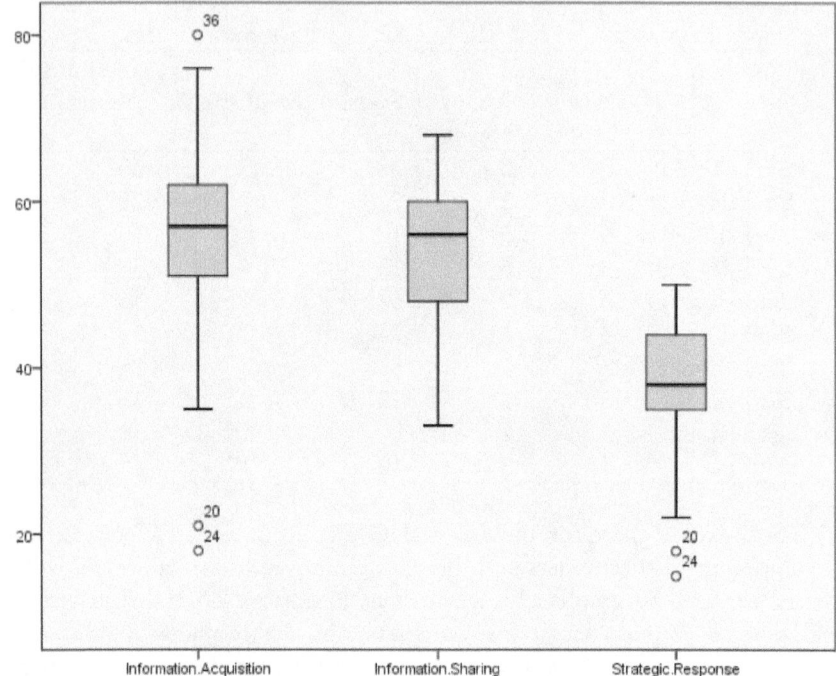

Figure 2. Boxplot graph of the outcomes for each global market orientation factor.

Cultural Intelligence Scale (CQS)

Table 13 presents the descriptive statistics for each of the CQS questions. The CQS survey instrument appears in Appendix D. A seven-ranking Likert scale was used, ranging from 1 (*strongly disagree*) to 7 (*strongly agree*), to assess individual cultural intelligence from the perspective of the participant's personal experience. The scale items have strong psychometric properties, comprising four items for metacognitive measurement, six items for cognitive measurement, five items for motivational measurement, and five items for behavioral measurement (Ang et al., 2007; Van Dyne, Ang, & Koh, 2009).

The survey question receiving the highest mean score for strongest (positive) agreement, 5.95, was question 39: *I enjoy interacting with people from different cultures.* This question focused on the motivational cultural intelligence factor. The survey questions with the lowest mean scores were questions 34 (2.76), 36 (3.05), and 38 (2.92). Question 34 stated: *I know the rules (e.g., vocabulary, grammar) of other languages.* Question 36 stated: *I know the marriage systems of other cultures.* Question 38 stated: *I know the rules for expressing non-verbal behaviors in other cultures.* These three questions with the lowest mean scores all are focused on individual cultural intelligence knowledge (the cognitive cultural intelligence factor). Question 39, which had the highest mean score, also had the lowest standard deviation (1.04). The question with the lowest mean score detailed earlier (question 34) had the second lowest standard deviation of responses, 1.17. The highest standard deviation of responses was 1.95 for behavioral cultural intelligence-focused question 48, which stated: *I alter my facial expressions when a cross-cultural interaction requires it.* The overall mean of the CQS survey sample was 4.34 over the 7-point scale with a standard deviation of 1.57.

Table 13 included coefficients that indicated symmetrical distribution in almost all CQS responses. As discussed earlier, discernable skewness exists if the absolute value of the skewness coefficient is less than two times the associated standard error. Questions 13, 14, and 15 (all motivational CQ factor questions) had very minor distribution skewness. Kurtosis coefficients did not indicate any abnormally sharp distribution peaks.

Table 13
Cultural Intelligence Scale Descriptive Statistics

Question	Min.	Max.	Mean	Std. Dev.	Skewness*	Kurtosis**
29	2	7	5.32	1.56	-0.694	-0.432
30	2	7	5.21	1.45	-0.499	-0.475
31	2	7	5.18	1.56	-0.686	-0.298
32	2	7	4.66	1.49	-0.143	-0.695
33	1	7	3.13	1.68	0.504	-0.661
34	1	5	2.76	1.17	-0.254	-1.070
35	1	7	3.71	1.58	-0.148	-0.714
36	1	6	3.05	1.80	0.181	-1.364
37	1	6	3.37	1.48	0.007	-1.140
38	1	6	2.92	1.38	0.343	-0.388
39	3	7	5.95	1.04	-0.960	0.552
40	2	7	5.18	1.57	-0.891	-0.113
41	1	7	5.18	1.43	-0.810	0.952
42	1	7	4.05	1.72	-0.086	-0.869
43	1	7	4.89	1.33	-0.668	1.015
44	1	7	4.34	1.92	-0.276	-1.088
45	1	7	4.42	1.80	-0.352	-1.025
46	1	7	4.92	1.78	-0.668	-0.351
47	1	7	4.50	1.70	-0.501	-0.249
48	1	7	4.00	1.95	-0.233	-0.977
Total			4.34	1.57	-0.342	-0.470

* Skewness Standard Error = 0.383
** Kurtosis Standard Error = 0.750

Table 14 presents analysis for each of the CQS questions among the seven available responses ranging from *Strongly Disagree (1)* to *Strongly Agree (7)*. The table defines each question with the appropriate Cultural Intelligence factor, namely Metacognitive CQ, Cognitive CQ, Motivational CQ, and Behavioral CQ.

Table 14
CQS Question Response Analysis and Factor

Q.	CQ Factor	Strongly Disagree (1)	(2)	(3)	(4)	(5)	(6)	Strongly Agree (7)
29	Metacognitive CQ	0	3	2	6	7	9	11
30	Metacognitive CQ	0	2	3	6	10	8	9
31	Metacognitive CQ	0	4	1	6	9	9	9
32	Metacognitive CQ	0	4	4	9	10	6	5
33	Cognitive CQ	7	9	8	5	5	3	1
34	Cognitive CQ	8	6	12	11	1	0	0
35	Cognitive CQ	4	6	5	10	9	3	1
36	Cognitive CQ	13	2	7	6	6	4	0
37	Cognitive CQ	4	9	7	7	9	2	0
38	Cognitive CQ	7	8	10	9	2	2	0
39	Motivational CQ	0	0	1	3	6	15	13
40	Motivational CQ	0	5	0	6	6	14	7
41	Motivational CQ	1	1	2	5	14	7	8
42	Motivational CQ	3	5	7	6	9	5	3
43	Motivational CQ	1	1	2	9	13	8	4
44	Behavioral CQ	3	7	2	5	10	5	6
45	Behavioral CQ	2	6	4	5	8	9	4
46	Behavioral CQ	2	3	3	4	11	6	9
47	Behavioral CQ	3	3	2	9	11	5	5
48	Behavioral CQ	7	3	2	10	7	5	4

The boxplot chart for the CQS data (see Figure 3) was developed to further understand the distribution and data values for respondent cultural intelligence. As is evident in Figure 3, the boxplot showed symmetrical distribution for three of the four cultural intelligence factors (metacognitive CQ, motivational CQ, and behavioral CQ). The boxplot shows a slight right skewed distribution (lower values) for the cognitive CQ factor. The chart clarified the skewness values in Table 13. The skewness coefficient indicated minor skewness for the motivational CQ factor; however, the boxplots graphically indicated distribution symmetry. Similarly, the skewness coefficient indicated no skewness for the cognitive CQ factor; however, the boxplots graphically indicated a slight right skewed distribution.

Based on the Figure 3 boxplot, the cognitive CQ factor had a range of 27 and interquartile range of 11. The metacognitive CQ factor had a range of 19 and interquartile range of 9. The motivational CQ factor had a range of 22 and an interquartile range of 7. The behavioral CQ factor had a range of 27 and an interquartile range of 8. The motivational CQ factor had the highest scores and cognitive CQ factor has the lowest scores out of all the cultural intelligence factors. Additionally, Figure 3 revealed no outlier cases for any cultural intelligence factor, which indicated no abnormal outcomes. Because there were no outlier cases, all cases were used in the research study.

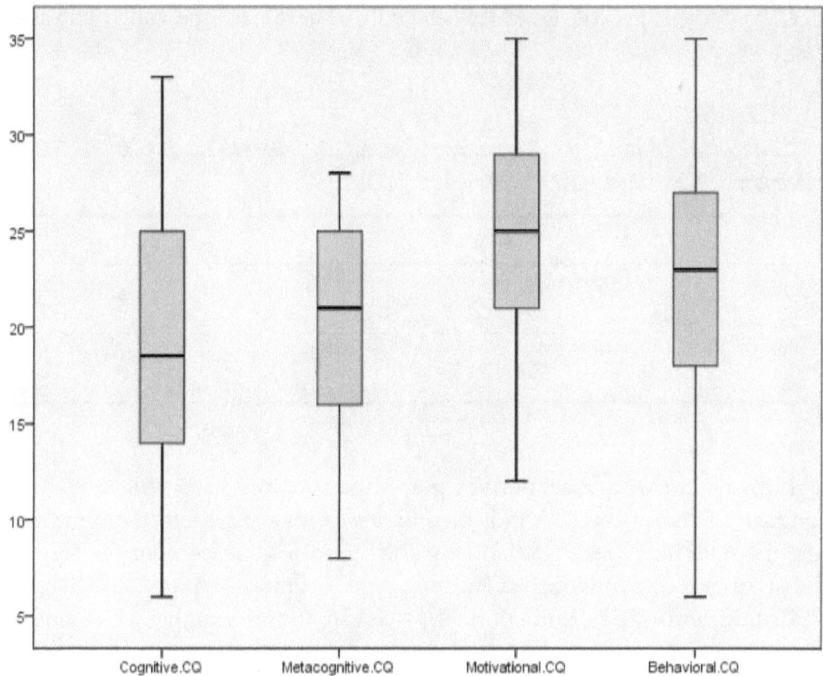

Figure 3. Boxplot graph of the outcomes for each cultural intelligence factor.

Hypotheses Test Results
Hypothesis 1

The following hypothesis and null hypothesis were tested:

H_{O1}: There is no significant relationship between cognitive cultural intelligence and global market information acquisition.

H_{A1}: There is a significant relationship between cognitive cultural intelligence and global market information acquisition.

The cognitive cultural intelligence factor from the CQS instrument (Ang et al., 2007; Van Dyne, Ang, & Koh, 2009) was tested for correlation with the market information acquisition factor from the I-MARKOR instrument (Schlosser, 2004; Schlosser & McNaughton, 2009) among participating global decision makers. The cognitive cultural intelligence factor score was an aggregate of six questions from the CQS instrument (Ang et al., 2007; Van Dyne, Ang, & Koh, 2009). The global market information acquisition factor score was an aggregate of eight questions from the I-MARKOR instrument (Schlosser, 2004; Schlosser & McNaughton, 2009). As shown in Table 15, a statistically significant relationship ($r = 0.331$, $p=0.042$) was observed between total cognitive cultural intelligence ($M = 3.16$, $SD = 1.54$, $N = 38$) and total global market information acquisition ($M = 3.40$, $SD = 1.18$, $N = 38$) at a .05 level (two-tailed). Therefore, the null hypothesis ($H_{\emptyset 1}$) was rejected.

Table 15

Correlation Matrix for Cognitive Cultural Intelligence and Global Market Information Acquisition Factors

			Cognitive CQ	Information Acquisition
Spearman's rho (ρ)	Cognitive CQ	Correlation Coefficient	1.000	.331*
		Sig. (2-tailed)	.	.042
		N	38	38
	Information Acquisition	Correlation Coefficient	.331*	1.000
		Sig. (2-tailed)	.042	.
		N	38	38

* Correlation is significant at the 0.05 level (2-tailed).

Figure 4 presents a scatterplot graph that demonstrates this statistically significant relationship. As indicated by the point scatter and the upward fit line, there exists a weak ($r=0.331$), positive monotonic correlation between global market information acquisition and cognitive cultural intelligence. The coefficient of determination (R^2) = 0.176 and means that 17.6% of the variability in the cognitive factor scale was explained by the variability in the information acquisition factor scale.

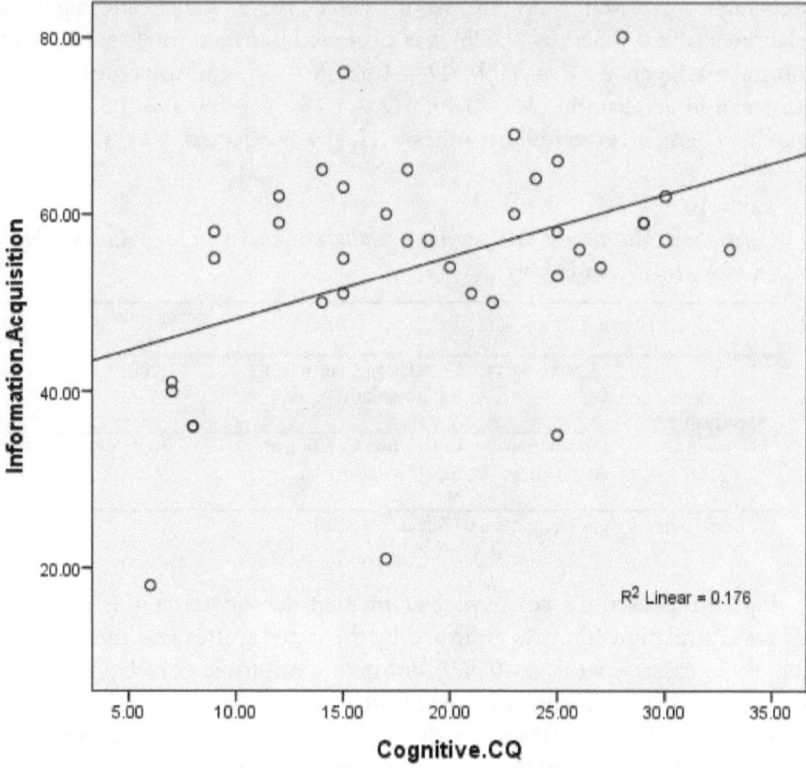

Figure 4. Scatterplot graph of the correlation between cognitive cultural intelligence and global market information acquisition, presenting a relationship found to be statistically significant.

Hypothesis 2

The following hypothesis and null hypothesis were tested:

H_{O2}: There is no significant relationship between metacognitive cultural intelligence and global market information acquisition.

H_{A2}: There is a significant relationship between metacognitive cultural intelligence and global market information acquisition.

The metacognitive cultural intelligence factor from the CQS instrument (Ang et al., 2007; Van Dyne, Ang, & Koh, 2009) was tested for correlation with the market information acquisition factor from the I-MARKOR instrument (Schlosser, 2004; Schlosser & McNaughton, 2009) among participating global decision makers. The metacognitive cultural intelligence factor score was an aggregate of four questions from the CQS instrument (Ang et al., 2007; Van Dyne, Ang, & Koh, 2009). The global market information acquisition factor score was an aggregate of eight questions from the I-MARKOR instrument (Schlosser, 2004; Schlosser &

McNaughton, 2009). As shown in Table 16, a statistically significant relationship ($r = 0.360$, $p=0.026$) was observed between total metacognitive cultural intelligence ($M = 5.09$, $SD = 1.52$, $N = 38$) and total global market information acquisition ($M = 3.40$, $SD = 1.18$, $N = 38$) at a .05 level (two-tailed). Therefore, the null hypothesis (H_{O2}) was rejected.

Table 16
Correlation Matrix for Metacognitive Cultural Intelligence and Global Market Information Acquisition Factors

			Metacognitive CQ	Information Acquisition
Spearman's rho (ρ)	Metacognitive CQ	Correlation Coefficient	1.000	.360*
		Sig. (2-tailed)	.	.026
		N	38	38
	Information Acquisition	Correlation Coefficient	.360*	1.000
		Sig. (2-tailed)	.026	.
		N	38	38

* Correlation is significant at the 0.05 level (2-tailed).

Figure 5 presents a scatterplot graph that demonstrates this statistically significant relationship. As indicated by the point scatter and the upward fit line, there exists a weak ($r=0.360$), positive monotonic correlation between global market information acquisition and metacognitive cultural intelligence. The coefficient of determination (R^2) = 0.080 and indicates that 8.0% of the variability in the metacognitive factor scale was explained by the variability in the information acquisition factor scale.

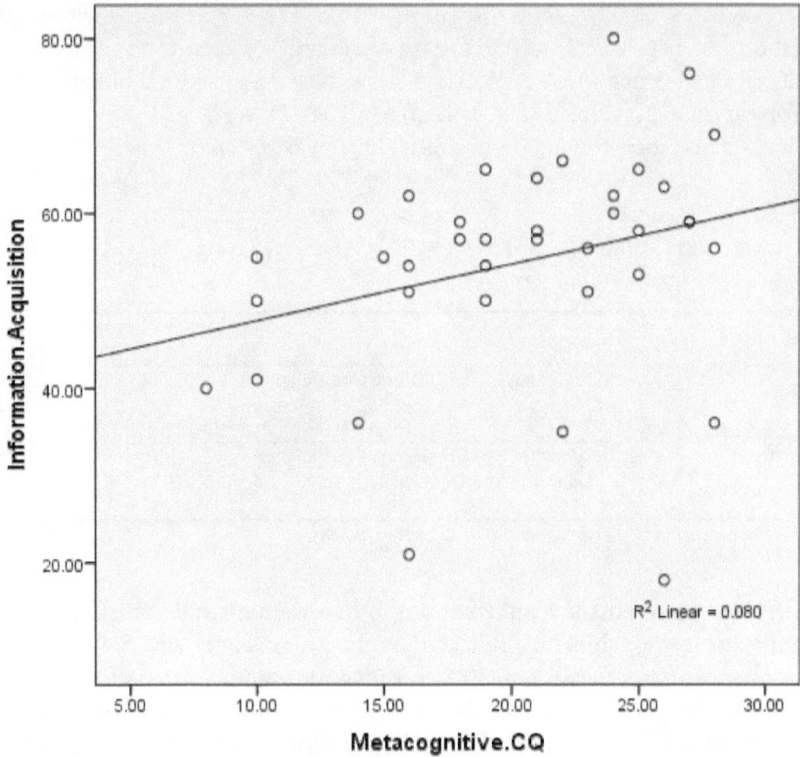

Figure 5. Scatterplot graph of the correlation between metacognitive cultural intelligence and global market information acquisition, presenting a relationship found to be statistically significant.

Hypothesis 3

The following hypothesis and null hypothesis were tested:

H_{O3}: There is no significant relationship between motivational cultural intelligence and global market information acquisition.

H_{A3}: There is a significant relationship between motivational cultural intelligence and global market information acquisition.

The motivational cultural intelligence factor from the CQS instrument (Ang et al., 2007; Van Dyne, Ang, & Koh, 2009) was tested for correlation with the market information acquisition factor from the I-MARKOR instrument (Schlosser, 2004; Schlosser & McNaughton, 2009) among participating global decision makers. The motivational cultural intelligence factor score was an aggregate of five questions from the CQS instrument (Ang et al., 2007; Van Dyne, Ang, & Koh, 2009). The global market information acquisition factor score was an aggregate of eight questions from the I-MARKOR instrument (Schlosser, 2004; Schlosser &

McNaughton, 2009). As shown in Table 17, a statistically significant relationship ($r = 0.390$, $p=0.016$) was observed between total motivational cultural intelligence ($M = 5.05$, $SD = 1.55$, $N = 38$) and total global market information acquisition ($M = 3.40$, $SD = 1.18$, $N = 38$) at a .05 level (two-tailed). Therefore, the null hypothesis ($H_{Ø3}$) was rejected.

Table 17

Correlation Matrix for Motivational Cultural Intelligence and Global Market Information Acquisition Factors

			Motivational CQ	Information Acquisition
Spearman's rho (ρ)	Motivational CQ	Correlation Coefficient	1.000	.390*
		Sig. (2-tailed)	.	.016
		N	38	38
	Information Acquisition	Correlation Coefficient	.390*	1.000
		Sig. (2-tailed)	.016	.
		N	38	38

* Correlation is significant at the 0.05 level (2-tailed).

Figure 6 presents a scatterplot graph that demonstrates this statistically significant relationship. As indicated by the point scatter and the upward fit line, there exists a weak ($r=0.390$), positive monotonic correlation between global market information acquisition and motivational cultural intelligence. The coefficient of determination $(R^2) = 0.176$ and signifies that 17.6% of the variability in the motivational factor scale was explained by the variability in the information acquisition factor scale.

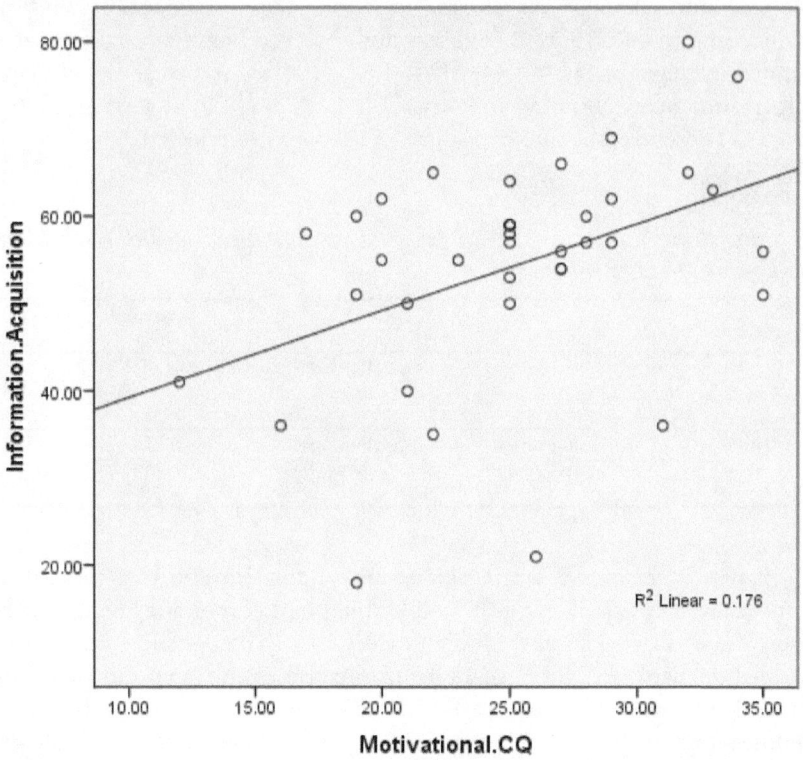

Figure 6. Scatterplot graph of the correlation between motivational cultural intelligence and global market information acquisition, presenting a relationship found to be statistically significant.

Hypothesis 4

The following hypothesis and null hypothesis were tested:

H_{O4}: There is no significant relationship between behavioral cultural intelligence and global market information acquisition.

H_{A4}: There is a significant relationship between behavioral cultural intelligence and global market information acquisition.

The behavioral cultural intelligence factor from the CQS instrument (Ang et al., 2007; Van Dyne, Ang, & Koh, 2009) was tested for correlation with the market information acquisition factor from the I-MARKOR instrument (Schlosser, 2004; Schlosser & McNaughton, 2009) among participating global decision makers. The behavioral cultural intelligence factor score was an aggregate of five questions from the CQS instrument (Ang et al., 2007; Van Dyne, Ang, & Koh, 2009). The global market information acquisition factor score was an aggregate of eight questions from the I-MARKOR instrument (Schlosser, 2004; Schlosser &

McNaughton, 2009). As shown in Table 18, a statistically significant relationship ($r = 0.218$, $p=0.189$) was not observed between total behavioral cultural intelligence ($M = 4.44$, $SD = 1.84$, $N = 38$) and total global market information acquisition ($M = 3.40$, $SD = 1.18$, $N = 38$) at a .05 level (two-tailed). Therefore, the null hypothesis (H_{O4}) was not rejected.

Table 18
Correlation Matrix for Behavioral Cultural Intelligence and Global Market Information Acquisition Factors

			Behavioral CQ	Information Acquisition
Spearman's rho (ρ)	Behavioral CQ	Correlation Coefficient	1.000	.218
		Sig. (2-tailed)	.	.189
		N	38	38
	Information Acquisition	Correlation Coefficient	.218	1.000
		Sig. (2-tailed)	.189	.
		N	38	38

Figure 7 presents a scatterplot graph of this relationship, though not statistically significant. As indicated by the point scatter and the upward fit line, there exists an extremely weak ($r=0.218$), positive monotonic correlation between global market information acquisition and behavioral cultural intelligence. The coefficient of determination (R^2) = 0.030 and denotes that 3.0% of the variability in the behavioral factor scale was explained by the variability in the information acquisition factor scale.

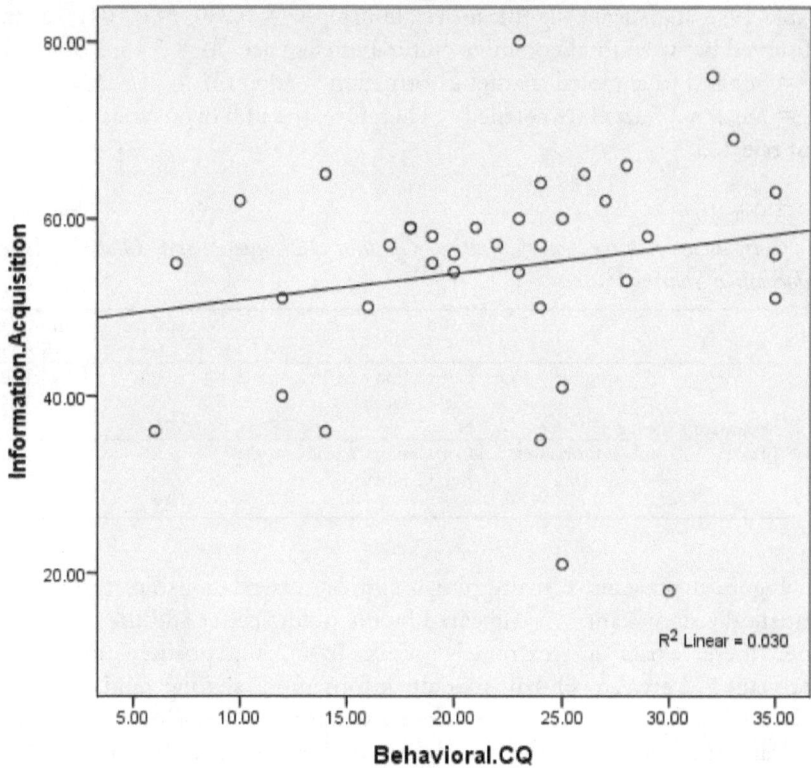

Figure 7. Scatterplot graph of the correlation between behavioral cultural intelligence and global market information acquisition, presenting a relationship found to be statistically significant.

Hypothesis 5

The following hypothesis and null hypothesis were tested:

$H_{Ø5}$: There is no significant relationship between cognitive cultural intelligence and global market information sharing.

H_{A5}: There is a significant relationship between cognitive cultural intelligence and global market information sharing.

The cognitive cultural intelligence factor from the CQS instrument (Ang et al., 2007; Van Dyne, Ang, & Koh, 2009) was tested for correlation with the market information sharing factor from the I-MARKOR instrument (Schlosser, 2004; Schlosser & McNaughton, 2009) among participating global decision makers. The cognitive cultural intelligence factor score was an aggregate of six questions from the CQS instrument (Ang et al., 2007; Van Dyne, Ang, & Koh, 2009). The global market information sharing factor score was an aggregate of seven questions from the I-MARKOR instrument (Schlosser, 2004; Schlosser & McNaughton, 2009). As shown in

Table 19, a statistically significant relationship ($r = 0.230$, $p=0.164$) was not observed between total cognitive cultural intelligence ($M = 3.16$, $SD = 1.54$, $N = 38$) and total global market information sharing ($M = 3.89$, $SD = 1.00$, $N = 38$) at a .05 level (two-tailed). Therefore, the null hypothesis (H_{O5}) was not rejected.

Table 19

Correlation Matrix for Cognitive Cultural Intelligence and Global Market Information Sharing Factors

			Cognitive CQ	Information Sharing
Spearman's rho (ρ)	Cognitive CQ	Correlation Coefficient	1.000	.230
		Sig. (2-tailed)	.	.164
		N	38	38
	Information Sharing	Correlation Coefficient	.230	1.000
		Sig. (2-tailed)	.164	.
		N	38	38

Figure 8 presents a scatterplot graph of this relationship, though not statistically significant. As indicated by the point scatter and the upward fit line, there exists an extremely weak (r=0.230), positive monotonic correlation between global market information sharing and cognitive cultural intelligence. The coefficient of determination (R^2) = 0.045 and indicates that 4.5% of the variability in the cognitive factor scale was explained by the variability in the information sharing factor scale.

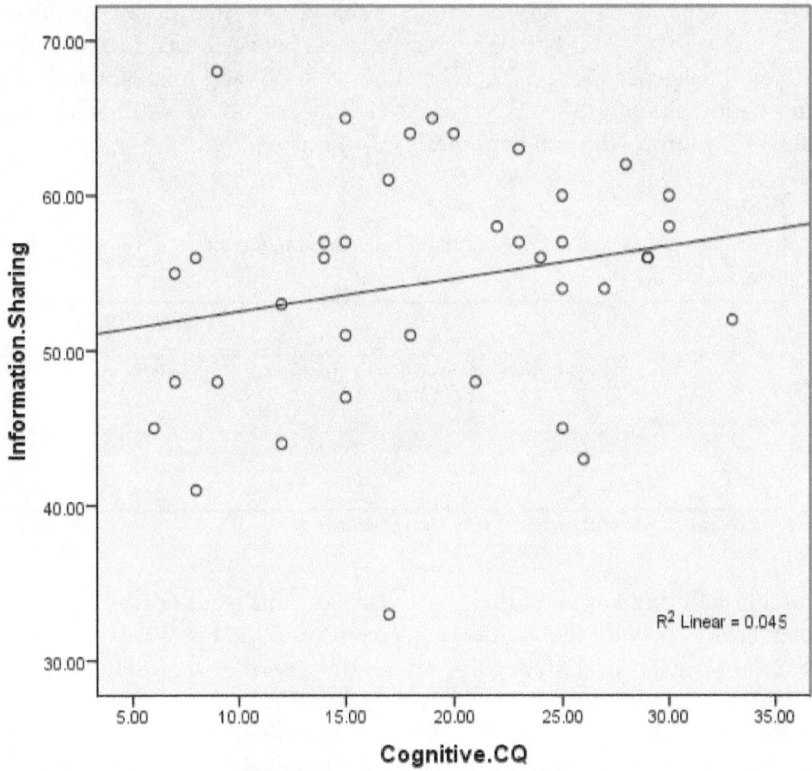

Figure 8. Scatterplot graph of the correlation between cognitive cultural intelligence and global market information sharing, though the relationship was not found to be statistically significant.

Hypothesis 6

The following hypothesis and null hypothesis were tested:

H_{O6}: There is no significant relationship between metacognitive cultural intelligence and global market information sharing.

H_{A6}: There is a significant relationship between metacognitive cultural intelligence and global market information sharing.

The metacognitive cultural intelligence factor from the CQS instrument (Ang et al., 2007; Van Dyne, Ang, & Koh, 2009) was tested for correlation with the market information sharing factor from the I-MARKOR instrument (Schlosser, 2004; Schlosser & McNaughton, 2009) among participating global decision makers. The metacognitive cultural intelligence factor score was an aggregate of four questions from the CQS instrument (Ang et al., 2007; Van Dyne, Ang, & Koh, 2009). The global market information sharing factor score was an aggregate of seven questions from the I-MARKOR instrument (Schlosser, 2004; Schlosser &

McNaughton, 2009). As shown in Table 20, a statistically significant relationship ($r = 0.342$, $p=0.035$) was observed between total metacognitive cultural intelligence ($M = 5.09$, $SD = 1.52$, $N = 38$) and total global market information sharing ($M = 3.89$, $SD = 1.00$, $N = 38$) at a .05 level (two-tailed). Therefore, the null hypothesis (H_{O6}) was rejected.

Table 20

Correlation Matrix for Metacognitive Cultural Intelligence and Global Market Information Sharing Factors

			Metacognitive CQ	Information Sharing
Spearman's rho (ρ)	Metacognitive CQ	Correlation Coefficient	1.000	.342*
		Sig. (2-tailed)	.	.035
		N	38	38
	Information Sharing	Correlation Coefficient	.342*	1.000
		Sig. (2-tailed)	.035	.
		N	38	38

* Correlation is significant at the 0.05 level (2-tailed).

Figure 9 presents a scatterplot graph of this statistically significant relationship. As indicated by the point scatter and the upward fit line, there exists a weak ($r=0.342$), positive monotonic correlation between global market information sharing and metacognitive cultural intelligence. The coefficient of determination (R^2) = 0.111 and signifies that 11.1% of the variability in the metacognitive factor scale was explained by the variability in the information sharing factor scale.

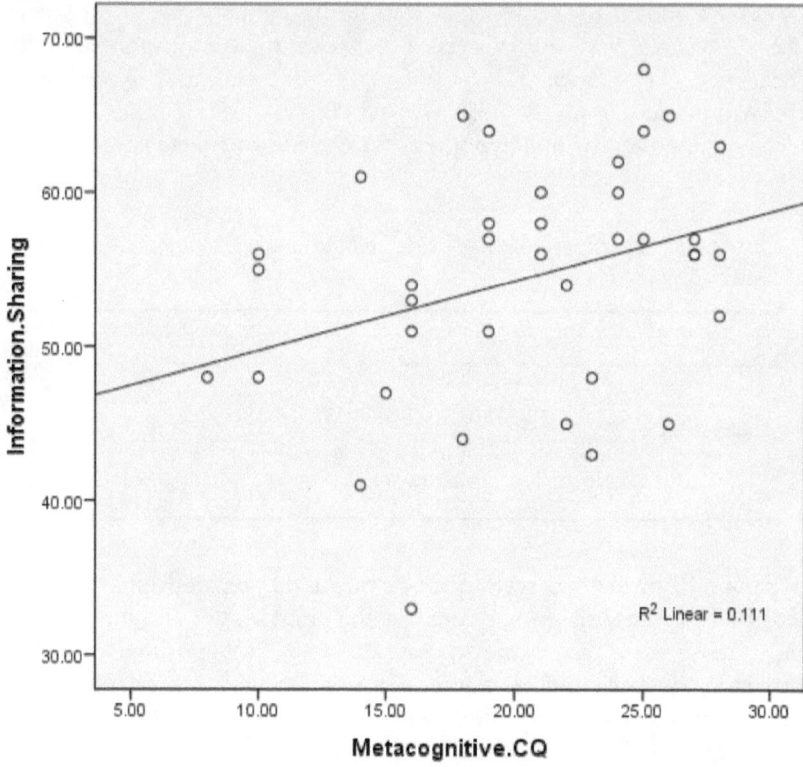

Figure 9. Scatterplot graph of the correlation between metacognitive cultural intelligence and global market information sharing, presenting a relationship found to be statistically significant.

Hypothesis 7

The following hypothesis and null hypothesis were tested:

H_{O7}: There is no significant relationship between motivational cultural intelligence and global market information sharing.

H_{A7}: There is a significant relationship between motivational cultural intelligence and global market information sharing.

The motivational cultural intelligence factor from the CQS instrument (Ang et al., 2007; Van Dyne, Ang, & Koh, 2009) was tested for correlation with the market information sharing factor from the I-MARKOR instrument (Schlosser, 2004; Schlosser & McNaughton, 2009) among participating global decision makers. The motivational cultural intelligence factor score was an aggregate of five questions from the CQS instrument (Ang et al., 2007; Van Dyne, Ang, & Koh, 2009). The global market information sharing factor score was an aggregate of seven questions from the I-MARKOR instrument (Schlosser, 2004; Schlosser & McNaughton,

2009). As shown in Table 21, a statistically significant relationship ($r = 0.224$, $p=0.176$) was not observed between total motivational cultural intelligence ($M = 5.05$, $SD = 1.55$, $N = 38$) and total global market information sharing ($M = 3.89$, $SD = 1.00$, $N = 38$) at a .05 level (two-tailed). Therefore, the null hypothesis (H_{O7}) was not rejected.

Table 21

Correlation Matrix for Motivational Cultural Intelligence and Global Market Information Sharing Factors

			Motivational CQ	Information Sharing
Spearman's rho (ρ)	Motivational CQ	Correlation Coefficient	1.000	.224
		Sig. (2-tailed)	.	.176
		N	38	38
	Information Sharing	Correlation Coefficient	.224	1.000
		Sig. (2-tailed)	.176	.
		N	38	38

Figure 10 presents a scatterplot graph of this relationship, though not statistically significant. As indicated by the point scatter and the upward fit line, there exists an extremely weak ($r=0.224$), positive monotonic correlation between global market information sharing and motivational cultural intelligence. The coefficient of determination (R^2) = 0.028 and means that 2.8% of the variability in the motivational factor scale was explained by the variability in the information sharing factor scale.

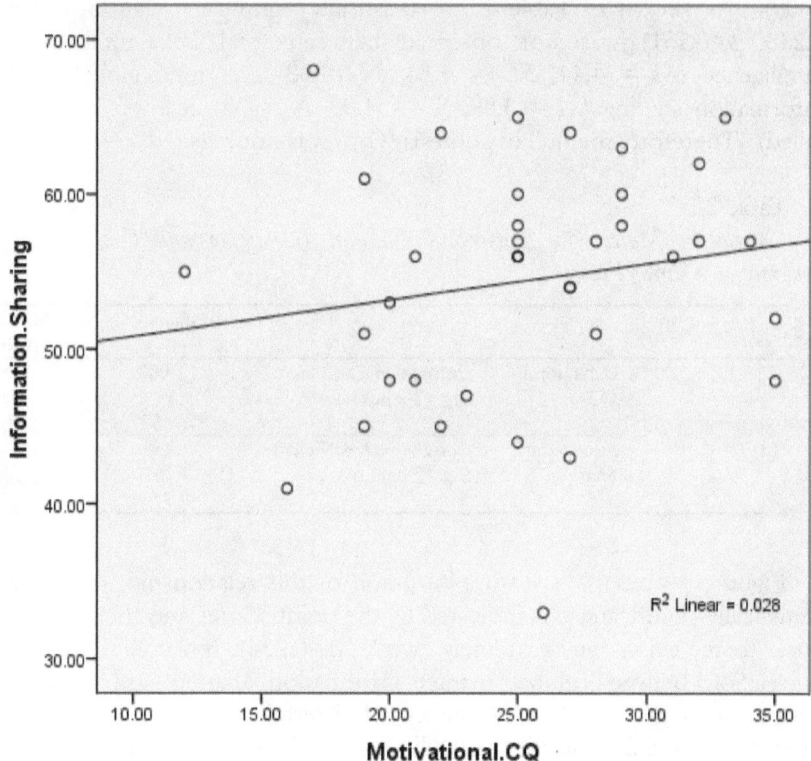

Figure 10. Scatterplot graph of the correlation between motivational cultural intelligence and global market information sharing, though the relationship was not found to be statistically significant.

Hypothesis 8

The following hypothesis and null hypothesis were tested:

H_{O8}: There is no significant relationship between behavioral cultural intelligence and global market information sharing.

H_{A8}: There is a significant relationship between behavioral cultural intelligence and global market information sharing.

The behavioral cultural intelligence factor from the CQS instrument (Ang et al., 2007; Van Dyne, Ang, & Koh, 2009) was tested for correlation with the market information sharing factor from the I-MARKOR instrument (Schlosser, 2004; Schlosser & McNaughton, 2009) among participating global decision makers. The behavioral cultural intelligence factor score was an aggregate of five questions from the CQS instrument (Ang et al., 2007; Van Dyne, Ang, & Koh, 2009). The global market information sharing factor score was an aggregate of seven questions from the I-MARKOR instrument (Schlosser, 2004; Schlosser & McNaughton,

2009). As shown in Table 22, a statistically significant relationship ($r = 0.238$, $p=0.151$) was not observed between total behavioral cultural intelligence ($M = 4.44$, $SD = 1.84$, $N = 38$) and total global market information sharing ($M = 3.89$, $SD = 1.00$, $N = 38$) at a .05 level (two-tailed). Therefore, the null hypothesis (H_{O8}) was not rejected.

Table 22

Correlation Matrix for Behavioral Cultural Intelligence and Global Market Information Sharing Factors

			Behavioral CQ	Information Sharing
Spearman's rho (ρ)	Behavioral CQ	Correlation Coefficient	1.000	.238
		Sig. (2-tailed)	.	.151
		N	38	38
	Information Sharing	Correlation Coefficient	.238	1.000
		Sig. (2-tailed)	.151	.
		N	38	38

Figure 11 presents a scatterplot graph of this relationship, though not statistically significant. As indicated by the point scatter and the upward fit line, there exists an extremely weak ($r=0.238$), positive monotonic correlation between global market information sharing and behavioral cultural intelligence. The coefficient of determination (R^2) = 0.068 and indicates that 6.8% of the variability in the behavioral factor scale was explained by the variability in the information sharing factor scale.

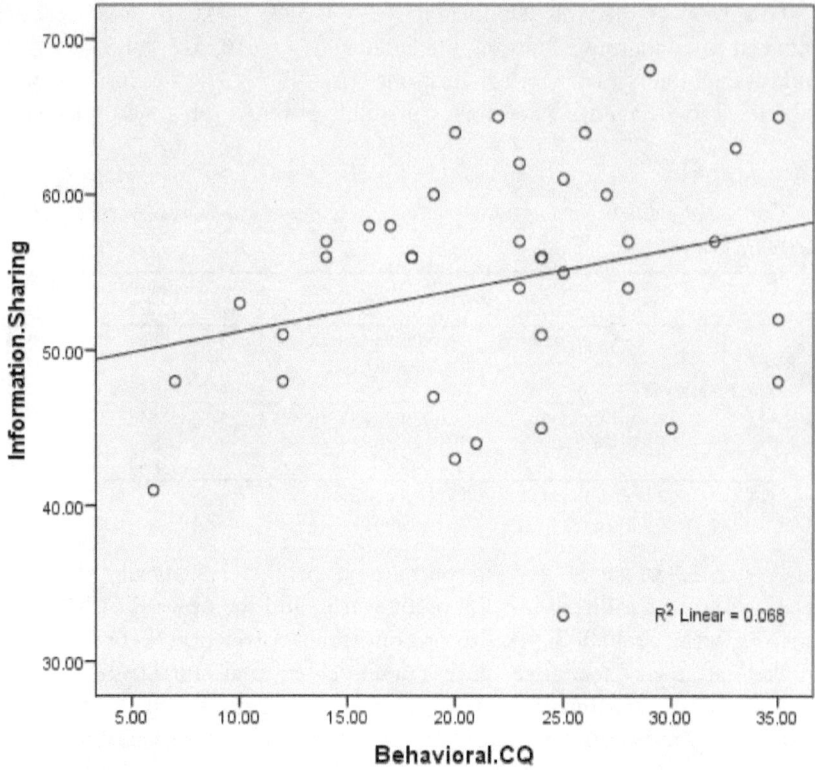

Figure 11. Scatterplot graph of the correlation between behavioral cultural intelligence and global market information sharing, though the relationship was not found to be statistically significant.

Hypothesis 9

The following hypothesis and null hypothesis were tested:

H_{O9}: There is no significant relationship between cognitive cultural intelligence and global market strategic response.

H_{A9}: There is a significant relationship between cognitive cultural intelligence and global market strategic response.

The cognitive cultural intelligence factor from the CQS instrument (Ang et al., 2007; Van Dyne, Ang, & Koh, 2009) was tested for correlation with the market strategic response factor from the I-MARKOR instrument (Schlosser, 2004; Schlosser & McNaughton, 2009) among participating global decision makers. The cognitive cultural intelligence factor score was an aggregate of six questions from the CQS instrument (Ang et al., 2007; Van Dyne, Ang, & Koh, 2009). The global market strategic response factor score was an aggregate of five questions from the I-MARKOR instrument (Schlosser, 2004; Schlosser & McNaughton, 2009). As shown in Table 23, a statistically significant relationship ($r = 0.388$, $p=0.016$) was observed between total cognitive cultural intelligence ($M = 3.16$, $SD = 1.54$, $N = 38$) and total global market strategic response ($M = 3.77$, $SD = 1.26$, $N = 38$) at a .05 level (two-tailed). Therefore, the null hypothesis (H_{O9}) was rejected.

Table 23

Correlation Matrix for Cognitive Cultural Intelligence and Global Market Strategic Response Factors

			Cognitive CQ	Strategic Response
Spearman's rho (ρ)	Cognitive CQ	Correlation Coefficient	1.000	.388*
		Sig. (2-tailed)	.	.016
		N	38	38
	Strategic Response	Correlation Coefficient	.388*	1.000
		Sig. (2-tailed)	.016	.
		N	38	38

* Correlation is significant at the 0.05 level (2-tailed).

Figure 12 presents a scatterplot graph of this statistically significant relationship. As indicated by the point scatter and the upward fit line, there exists a weak ($r=0.388$), positive monotonic correlation between global market strategic response and cognitive cultural intelligence. The coefficient of determination (R^2) = 0.207 and signifies that 20.7% of the variability in the cognitive factor scale was explained by the variability in the strategic response factor scale.

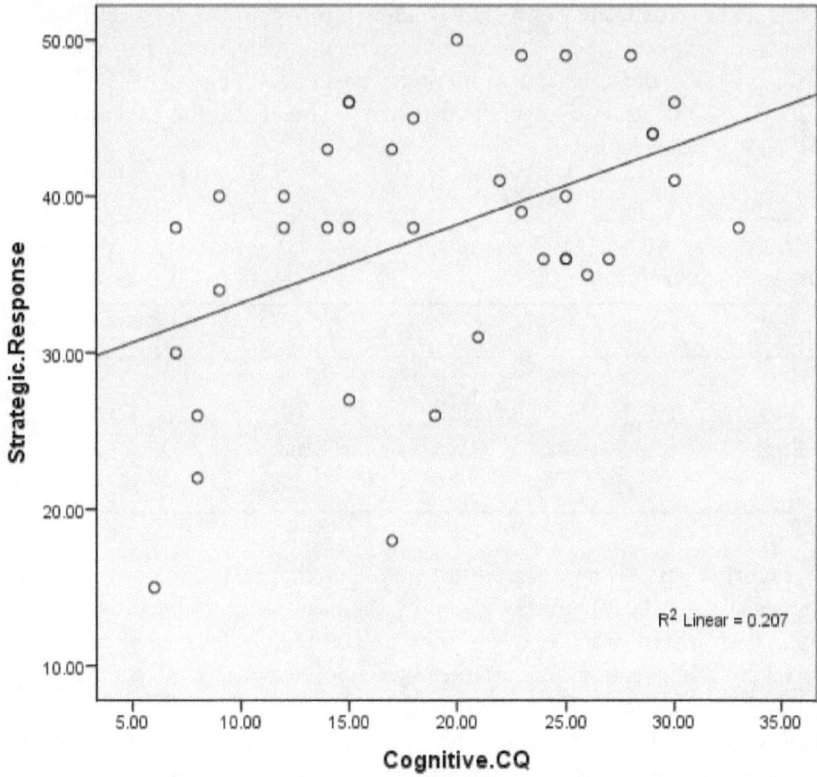

Figure 12. Scatterplot graph of the correlation between cognitive cultural intelligence and global market strategic response, presenting a relationship found to be statistically significant.

Hypothesis 10

The following hypothesis and null hypothesis were tested:

$H_{Ø10}$: There is no significant relationship between metacognitive cultural intelligence and global market strategic response.

H_{A10}: There is a significant relationship between metacognitive cultural intelligence and global market strategic response.

The metacognitive cultural intelligence factor from the CQS instrument (Ang et al., 2007; Van Dyne, Ang, & Koh, 2009) was tested for correlation with the market strategic response factor from the I-MARKOR instrument (Schlosser, 2004; Schlosser & McNaughton, 2009) among participating global decision makers. The metacognitive cultural intelligence factor score was an aggregate of four questions from the CQS instrument (Ang et al., 2007; Van Dyne, Ang, & Koh, 2009). The global market strategic response factor score was an aggregate of five questions from the I-MARKOR instrument (Schlosser, 2004; Schlosser & McNaughton, 2009). As shown in

Table 24, a statistically significant relationship ($r = 0.233$, $p=0.160$) was not observed between total metacognitive cultural intelligence ($M = 5.09$, $SD = 1.52$, $N = 38$) and total global market strategic response ($M = 3.77$, $SD = 1.26$, $N = 38$) at a .05 level (two-tailed). Therefore, the null hypothesis ($H_{\emptyset 10}$) was not rejected.

Table 24

Correlation Matrix for Metacognitive Cultural Intelligence and Global Market Strategic Response Factors

			Metacognitive CQ	Strategic Response
Spearman's rho (ρ)	Metacognitive CQ	Correlation Coefficient	1.000	.233
		Sig. (2-tailed)	.	.160
		N	38	38
	Strategic Response	Correlation Coefficient	.233	1.000
		Sig. (2-tailed)	.160	.
		N	38	38

Figure 13 presents a scatterplot graph of this relationship, though not statistically significant. As indicated by the point scatter and the upward fit line, there exists an extremely weak ($r=0.233$), positive monotonic correlation between global market strategic response and metacognitive cultural intelligence. The coefficient of determination (R^2) = 0.031 and denotes that 3.1% of the variability in the metacognitive factor scale was explained by the variability in the strategic response factor scale.

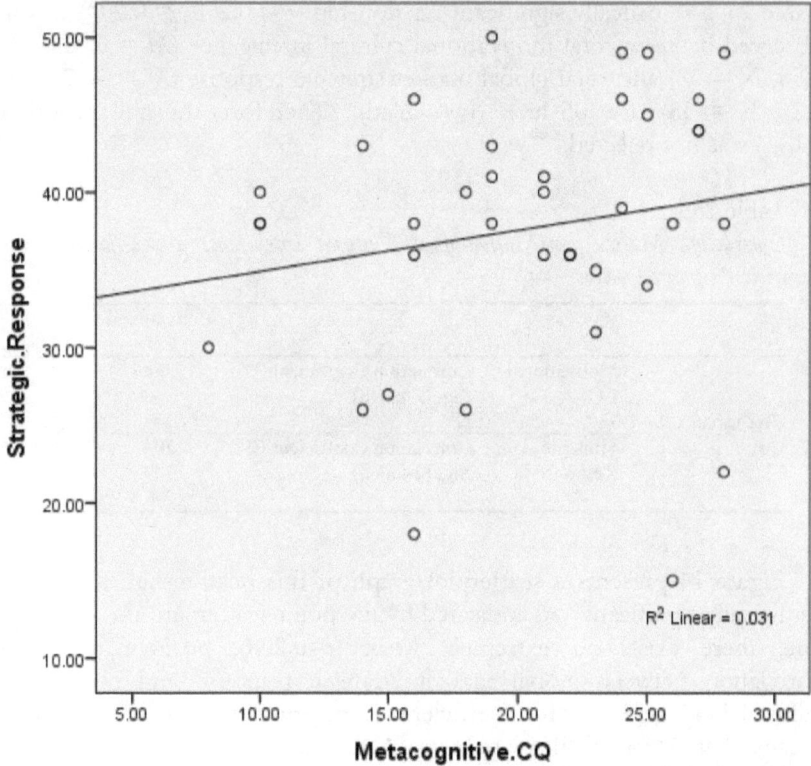

Figure 13. Scatterplot graph of the correlation between metacognitive cultural intelligence and global market strategic response, though the relationship was not found to be statistically significant.

Hypothesis 11

The following hypothesis and null hypothesis were tested:

$H_{Ø11}$: There is no significant relationship between motivational cultural intelligence and global market strategic response.

H_{A11}: There is a significant relationship between motivational cultural intelligence and global market strategic response.

The motivational cultural intelligence factor from the CQS instrument (Ang et al., 2007; Van Dyne, Ang, & Koh, 2009) was tested for correlation with the market strategic response factor from the I-MARKOR instrument (Schlosser, 2004; Schlosser & McNaughton, 2009) among participating global decision makers. The motivational cultural intelligence factor score was an aggregate of five questions from the CQS instrument (Ang et al., 2007; Van Dyne, Ang, & Koh, 2009). The global market strategic response factor score was an aggregate of five questions from the I-MARKOR instrument (Schlosser, 2004; Schlosser & McNaughton, 2009). As shown in

Table 25, a statistically significant relationship ($r = 0.208$, $p=0.209$) was not observed between total motivational cultural intelligence ($M = 5.05$, $SD = 1.55$, $N = 38$) and total global market strategic response ($M = 3.77$, $SD = 1.26$, $N = 38$) at a .05 level (two-tailed). Therefore, the null hypothesis ($H_{\emptyset 11}$) was not rejected.

Table 25

Correlation Matrix for Motivational Cultural Intelligence and Global Market Strategic Response Factors

			Motivational CQ	Strategic Response
Spearman's rho (ρ)	Motivational CQ	Correlation Coefficient	1.000	.208
		Sig. (2-tailed)	.	.209
		N	38	38
	Strategic Response	Correlation Coefficient	.208	1.000
		Sig. (2-tailed)	.209	.
		N	38	38

Figure 14 presents a scatterplot graph of this relationship, though not statistically significant. As indicated by the point scatter and the upward fit line, there exists an extremely weak ($r=0.208$), positive monotonic correlation between global market strategic response and motivational cultural intelligence. The coefficient of determination (R^2) = 0.038 and means that 3.8% of the variability in the motivational factor scale was explained by the variability in the strategic response factor scale.

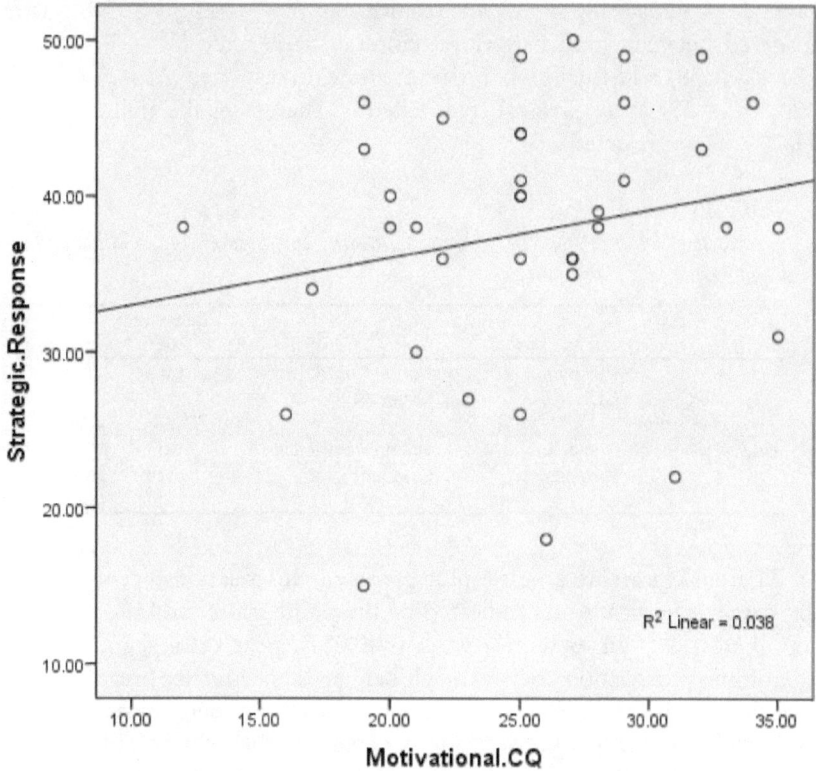

Figure 14. Scatterplot graph of the correlation between motivational cultural intelligence and global market strategic response, though the relationship was not found to be statistically significant.

Hypothesis 12

The following hypothesis and null hypothesis were tested:

H_{O12}: There is no significant relationship between behavioral cultural intelligence and global market strategic response.

H_{A12}: There is a significant relationship between behavioral cultural intelligence and global market strategic response.

The behavioral cultural intelligence factor from the CQS instrument (Ang et al., 2007; Van Dyne, Ang, & Koh, 2009) was tested for correlation with the market strategic response factor from the I-MARKOR instrument (Schlosser, 2004; Schlosser & McNaughton, 2009) among participating global decision makers. The behavioral cultural intelligence factor score was an aggregate of five questions from the CQS instrument (Ang et al., 2007; Van Dyne, Ang, & Koh, 2009). The global market strategic response factor score was an aggregate of five questions from the I-MARKOR instrument (Schlosser, 2004; Schlosser & McNaughton, 2009). As shown in

Table 26, a statistically significant relationship ($r = 0.017$, $p=0.918$) was not observed between total behavioral cultural intelligence ($M = 4.44$, $SD = 1.84$, $N = 38$) and total global market strategic response ($M = 3.77$, $SD = 1.26$, $N = 38$) at a .05 level (two-tailed). Therefore, the null hypothesis (H_{O12}) was not rejected.

Table 26

Correlation Matrix for Behavioral Cultural Intelligence and Global Market Strategic Response Factors

			Behavioral CQ	Strategic Response
Spearman's rho (ρ)	Behavioral CQ	Correlation Coefficient	1.000	.017
		Sig. (2-tailed)	.	.918
		N	38	38
	Strategic Response	Correlation Coefficient	.017	1.000
		Sig. (2-tailed)	.918	.
		N	38	38

Figure 15 presents a scatterplot graph of this relationship, though not statistically significant. As indicated by the point scatter and the upward fit line, there exists an extremely weak ($r=0.017$), near zero, slightly positive monotonic correlation between global market strategic response and behavioral cultural intelligence. The coefficient of determination (R^2) = 0.004 and signifies that 0.4% of the variability in the behavioral factor scale was explained by the variability in the strategic response factor scale.

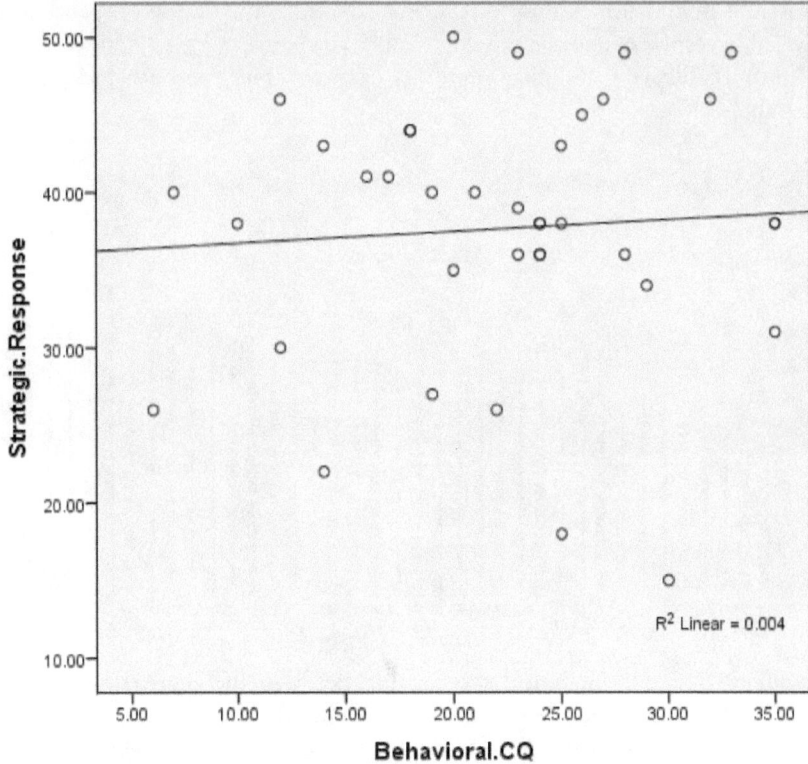

Figure 15. Scatterplot graph of the correlation between behavioral cultural intelligence and global market strategic response, though the relationship was not found to be statistically significant.

Relationship between Cultural Intelligence and Global Market Orientation

Figure 16 depicts the aggregate cultural intelligence and global-focused market orientation scores for each of the respondents (N=38). Scores for each variable are ranked independently from lowest (case 1) to highest (case 38). Thus, respondents may have a different case number for each variable depending on their placement among the collective aggregate variable scores. For example, case #10 under cultural intelligence and case #10 under global market orientation were likely different respondents. Aggregate scores are based on the instrument questions and available response choices. Based on the I-MARKOR instrument, each respondent could score a total of 200 possible points for global market orientation, based on 20 questions with two variations per question (*I should* and *I do*) and five available response choices ranging from 1 (*never*) to 5 (*almost always*). Based on the CQS instrument, each respondent could score a total of 140 possible points for cultural intelligence, based on 20 questions and seven available response choices ranging from 1 (*strongly disagree*) to 7 (*strongly agree*). Figure 16 displays a similar increase, case by case, for both independent variables.

Figure 16. The graphical relationship between the aggregate scores for both Global Market Orientation and Cultural Intelligence. Scores are ranked from lowest (case 1) to highest (case 38).

Table 27 contains descriptive statistics related to the aggregate scores of cultural intelligence and global market orientation among the respondent global decision makers. Global market orientation scores ranged from 72.00 to 191.00 based on a total possible score of 200. The mean aggregate score was 146.50 and the standard deviation was 25.47. Cultural intelligence scores ranged from 44.00 to 131.00 based on a total possible score of 140. The mean aggregate cultural intelligence score was 86.76 and standard deviation was 20.18.

Table 27
Cultural Intelligence and Global Market Orientation Descriptive Statistics

	N	Min.	Max.	Mean	Std. Dev.
Global Market Orientation	38	72.00	191.00	146.50	25.47
Cultural Intelligence	38	44.00	131.00	86.76	20.18

The boxplot chart for the aggregate score data (see Figure 17) was developed to further understand the distribution and data values for respondent global market orientation and cultural intelligence. As is evident in Figure 17, the boxplot showed nearly symmetrical distribution for cultural intelligence factors. The boxplot shows a slight left skewed distribution (higher values) for global market orientation.

Based on the Figure 17 boxplot, global market orientation aggregate score had a range of 85 and interquartile range of 30. The cultural intelligence aggregate score had a range of 82 and interquartile range of 24. Additionally, Figure 17 revealed outliers (Cases 20 and 24) for global market orientation only, which indicated those values are abnormal. Because these outlier cases had relevant outcomes for one of the global market orientation factors (information sharing) and for aggregate cultural intelligence, both cases were retained in the research study.

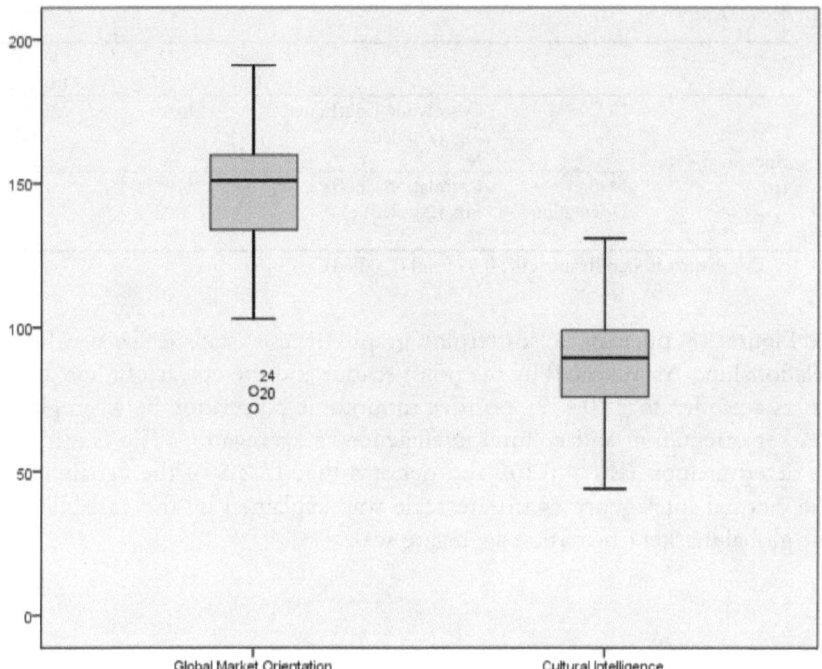

Figure 17. Boxplot graph of the aggregate scores for cultural intelligence and global market orientation.

The aggregate cultural intelligence score from the CQS instrument (Ang et al., 2007; Van Dyne, Ang, & Koh, 2009) was tested for correlation with the aggregate global-focused market orientation score from the I-MARKOR instrument (Schlosser, 2004; Schlosser & McNaughton, 2009) among participating global decision makers. The aggregate cultural intelligence score was an aggregate of all 20 questions from the CQS instrument (Ang et al., 2007; Van Dyne, Ang, & Koh, 2009). The global market orientation score was an aggregate of *I should* and *I do* variations of the 20 questions (totaling 40 responses per respondent) from the I-MARKOR instrument (Schlosser, 2004; Schlosser & McNaughton, 2009). As shown in Table 28, a statistically significant relationship ($r = 0.479$, $p=0.002$) was observed between total cultural intelligence ($M = 4.34$, $SD = 1.81$, $N = 38$) and total global market orientation ($M = 3.66$, $SD = 1.17$, $N = 38$) at a .05 level (two-tailed). Therefore, cultural intelligence and global market orientation as aggregate scores among global decision makers have positive, statistically significant correlation.

Table 28

Correlation Matrix for Cultural Intelligence and Global Market Orientation Aggregate Scores

			CQ	Market Orientation
Spearman's rho (ρ)	CQ	Correlation Coefficient	1.000	.479**
		Sig. (2-tailed)	.	.002
		N	38	38
	Market Orientation	Correlation Coefficient	.479**	1.000
		Sig. (2-tailed)	.002	.
		N	38	38

* Correlation is significant at the 0.05 level (2-tailed).

Figure 18 presents a scatterplot graph of this statistically significant relationship. As indicated by the point scatter and the upward fit line, there exists a moderate ($r=0.479$), positive monotonic correlation between global market orientation and cultural intelligence as aggregates. The coefficient of determination (R^2) = 0.162 and denotes that 16.2% of the variability in the cultural intelligence aggregate scale was explained by the variability in the global market orientation aggregate scale.

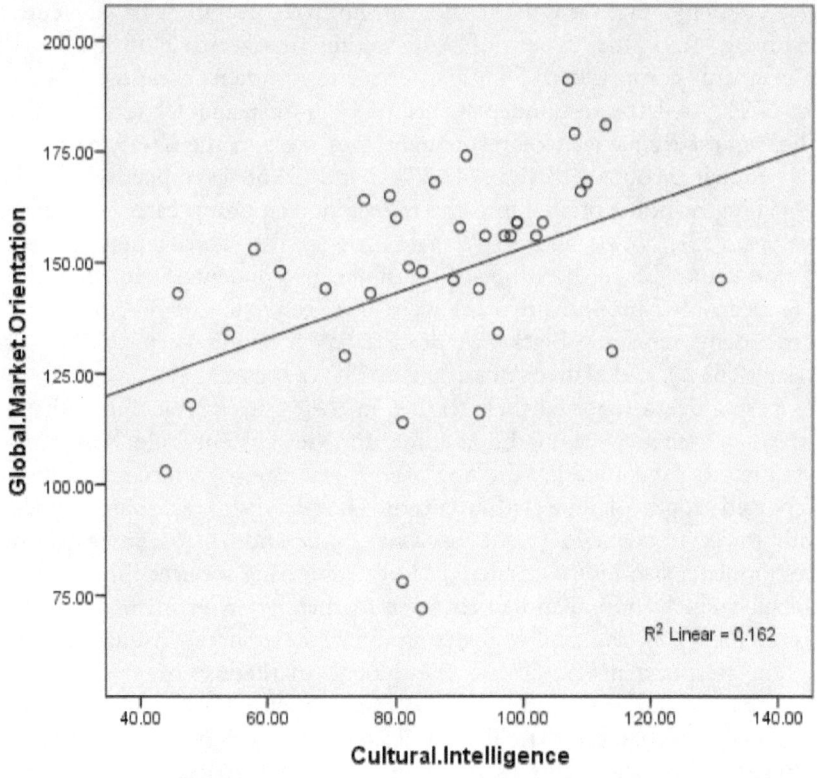

Figure 18. Scatterplot graph of the correlation between aggregate cultural intelligence and aggregate global market orientation, presenting a relationship found to be statistically significant.

Summary

Chapter 4 included the descriptive and statistical analyses of the collected data from participating respondents (N=38) using two validated survey instruments and targeted demographic questions through the survey website, *surveymonkey.com*. Specifically, all respondents completed the online demographic questions and online versions of the Cultural Intelligence Scale (Ang et al., 2007; Van Dyne, Ang, & Koh, 2009) and I-MARKOR (Schlosser, 2004; Schlosser & McNaughton, 2009) instruments. The presented results of this study included analysis of demographic data, hypotheses testing, and aggregate Cultural Intelligence and Global Market Orientation scores. Demographic descriptive statistics, hypotheses testing, correlation analysis, data plotting, and aggregate score analysis was conducted using a combination of Microsoft Excel and IBM's SPSS Statistics Version 21 software.

Demographic data were collected, including the respondent's gender, age, ethnicity, race, length in the current role, length with the current company, and the types of engineering marketed globally. Male respondents comprised 65.79% and female respondents comprised 34.21%, and 97.37% of the respondents were of Non-Hispanic / Latino ethnicity. The highest frequencies of respondent ages were in the *21-30, 51-60,* and *over 80* age groups (18.42%, 47.37%, and 23.68% respectively). The remaining respondents fell into the remaining age group categories, except the *under 21, 31-40* and *61-70* age groups, for which there were no respondents. More than four-fifths of the respondents were of White / Caucasian / European descent with the remaining one fifth of the respondents reporting Black / African (2.63%), South Asian (5.26%), East Asian (2.63%), and Native American (2.63%) descent.

Respondents reported their tenures in their current role and with their current company. Length of time in the current role was closely distributed, except under the *less than 1 year* category (no respondents). Reported length of time with a current company was distributed similarly with lower frequencies in the *less than 1 year* and *16-20 years* categories. Respondents also indicated the types of engineering services they marketed globally, which more than half reported marketing environmental (71.05%), power (60.53%), and civil engineering (55.26%) services. A quarter to half of the respondents indicated the global marketing of transportation (50.00%), green/sustainability (47.37%), structural (47.37%), electrical (44.74%), mechanical (31.58%), and geotechnical (26.32%) engineering services. No respondents reported marketing aerospace, biomolecular, or nanoengineering services. The remaining 15 engineering categories were reported by less than a quarter of the respondents.

Following the demographic data analysis, each hypothesis was tested for statistical significance using calculation and analysis of the Spearman's rho (ρ) correlation coefficient. Data plotting supported statistical results and visually demonstrated positive, monotonic correlation for each hypothesis, from extremely weak correlations ($r< 0.30$) to moderate correlations ($0.40<r< 0.60$). Scatterplots of each hypothesis illustrated the statistically significant and non-statistically significant relationships. The scatterplots included coefficients of determination (R^2) and the associated fit line to illustrate data variations.

Table 29 provides a summary of the research hypotheses testing results. As indicated, statistically significant relationships were observed between global market information acquisition and the cognitive, metacognitive, and motivational cultural intelligence factors (H_{A1}, H_{A2}, and H_{A3} respectively). Statistically significant relationships were also observed between global market information sharing and metacognitive cultural intelligence (H_{A6}), and global market strategic response and cognitive cultural intelligence (H_{A9}). For these observed statistically significant relationships, the null hypotheses were rejected. However, the remaining hypotheses (H_{A4}, H_{A5}, H_{A7}, H_{A8}, H_{A10}, H_{A11}, and H_{A12}) had no statistically significant relationships observed and resulted in the associated null hypotheses not being rejected.

Table 29
Results from Hypotheses Testing

Null Hypothesis	Statistical Significance	Result
H_{01}: There is no significant relationship between cognitive cultural intelligence and global market information acquisition.	$p < 0.05$	Null Hypothesis was rejected.
H_{02}: There is no significant relationship between metacognitive cultural intelligence and global market information acquisition.	$p < 0.05$	Null Hypothesis was rejected.
H_{03}: There is no significant relationship between motivational cultural intelligence and global market information acquisition.	$p < 0.05$	Null Hypothesis was rejected.
H_{04}: There is no significant relationship between behavioral cultural intelligence and global market information acquisition.	$p < 0.05$	Null Hypothesis was not rejected.
H_{05}: There is no significant relationship between cognitive cultural intelligence and global market information sharing.	$p < 0.05$	Null Hypothesis was not rejected.
H_{06}: There is no significant relationship between metacognitive cultural intelligence and global market information sharing.	$p < 0.05$	Null Hypothesis was rejected.
H_{07}: There is no significant relationship between motivational cultural intelligence and global market information sharing.	$p < 0.05$	Null Hypothesis was not rejected.
H_{08}: There is no significant relationship between behavioral cultural intelligence and global market information sharing.	$p < 0.05$	Null Hypothesis was not rejected.
H_{09}: There is no significant relationship between cognitive cultural intelligence and global market strategic response.	$p < 0.05$	Null Hypothesis was rejected.
H_{010}: There is no significant relationship between metacognitive cultural intelligence and global market strategic response	$p < 0.05$	Null Hypothesis was not rejected.
H_{011}: There is no significant relationship between motivational cultural intelligence and global market strategic response.	$p < 0.05$	Null Hypothesis was not rejected.
H_{012}: There is no significant relationship between behavioral cultural intelligence and global market strategic response.	$p < 0.05$	Null Hypothesis was not rejected.

After analyzing respondent demographics and testing all hypotheses, statistical focus turned to the collective global market orientation and cultural intelligence scores. Aggregate scores for cultural intelligence and global market orientation were calculated to assess whether a statistically significant relationship exists between both variables. Statistical analysis included calculations of descriptive analysis (including frequencies, mean, and standard deviations) and the Spearman rho (ρ) correlation coefficient. A statistically significant relationship ($r = 0.479$, $p=0.002$) was observed between total cultural intelligence ($M = 4.34$, $SD = 1.81$, $N = 38$) and total global market orientation ($M = 3.66$, $SD = 1.17$, $N = 38$) at a .05 level (two-tailed). A positive monotonic correlation exists between both aggregates. Boxplots and scatter plots supported this analysis and provided visual evidence of 16.2% variability between both independent variables' data.

The next and final section, Chapter 5, includes conclusions based on the research study findings and recommendations for future research, practice, and theory. The conclusions relate the findings to the research question, the hypotheses, and the study's literature review. The recommendations apply to how this study can be used or revised for further research in cultural intelligence and global market orientation. Recommendations also include suggestions for future practice and theory-based scholarly work. Chapter 5 also includes limitations to this study and the possible implications of this research to the areas of leadership, global engineering, global market orientation, and cultural intelligence.

FIVE

CONCLUSIONS AND RECCOMENDATIONS

The purpose of this quantitative correlational study was to determine any relationship that may exist between cultural intelligence and market orientation of decision makers at U.S.-based engineering firms entering the global marketplace. Measurement of the variables for the aggregate and individual factors of cultural intelligence occurred using the Cultural Intelligence Scale (Ang et al., 2007; Van Dyne, Ang, & Koh, 2009). The I-MARKOR (Schlosser, 2004; Schlosser & McNaughton, 2009) was used to measure the variable of global market orientation. The study sample included senior-level global engineering and marketing decision makers from U.S.-based engineering firms listed on ENR's Top 150 Global Design Firms and Top 200 International Design Firms listings.

Chapter 5 begins with study conclusions based on the research findings and data analysis presented in chapter 4. The chapter continues with a discussion about implications of the findings with relation to leadership, global market orientation, and cultural intelligence. The discussion advances to a review of study limitations. Finally, Chapter 5 concludes with recommendations for future research and practice.

Study Conclusions

The analyses of study findings indicated a significant relationship between cultural intelligence and global market orientation on the aggregate level, but presented various results as related to sub-elements of the variables from the study's research question and hypotheses. Figure 19 provides summary of the study findings. The figure illustrates the resultant significant and non-significant relationships among the factors of cultural intelligence and global market orientation. The figure also represents the other findings among aggregate cultural intelligence and aggregate global market orientation.

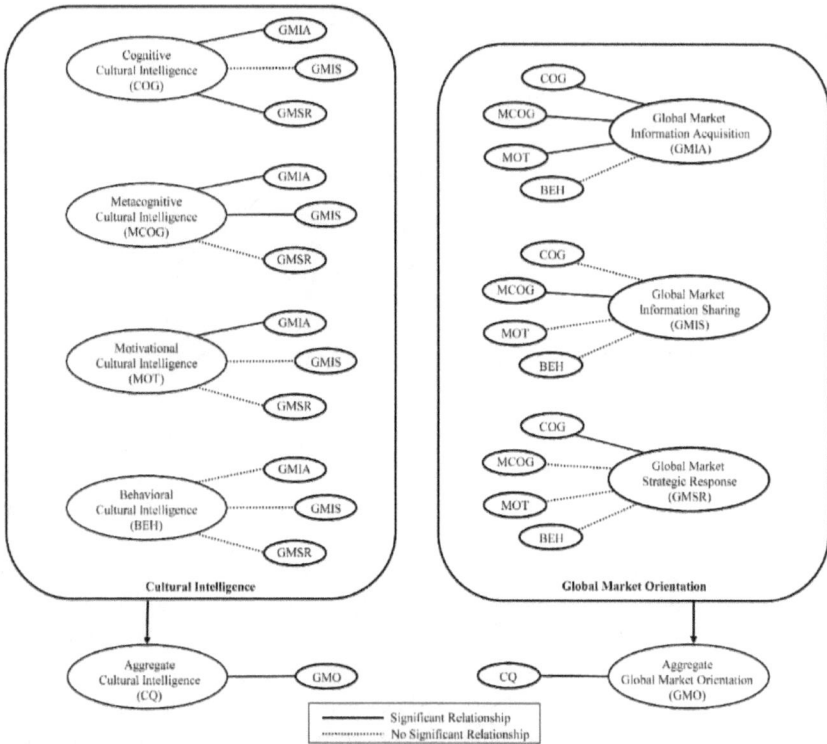

Figure 19. Study findings map showing significant and non-significant relationships.

The following subsections expand the discussion of founded relationships between the four factors of cultural intelligence to the three factors of global market orientation as uncovered by this study. Each subsection involves conclusions based on the study findings for a factor of cultural intelligence as related to all three global market orientation factors. The ultimate goals were to expand the study findings analysis and further expose the distinct relationships with regard to new and existing literature on the topics.

Cognitive Cultural Intelligence and Global Market Orientation Factors

The study findings, which are confirmed by literature, showed that cognitive cultural intelligence has a significant correlation to global market information acquisition and global market strategic response, while the findings showed no significant correlation to global market information sharing. From these findings, a conclusion is that a strong cognitive cultural intelligence pairs with how decision makers acquire and respond to global market information. Rockstuhl, Seiler, Ang, Van Dyne, and Annen (2011) contended that leaders with high cultural intelligence, particularly high cognitive abilities, reflect on and confirm their own assumptions about cultures to predict market expectations and intercultural interactions. This strong cognitive function better orients decision-makers with the target markets through evaluating the collected market information and devising a reasonable market response.

Decision-makers must wade through what they know, what they have experienced, and what they have heard about global market cultures to succeed in that market. Kim and Van Dyne (2012) concurred that individuals with lower cultural intelligence have the proclivity to engage in cultural stereotypes and "heard through the grapevine" decision-making that can ultimately cause conflicts, delay progress in culturally complex environments, and result in global leadership failure. A lack of progress within diverse environments can signify delays in market penetration. However, individuals with developed cultural intelligence have heightened cognitive aptitude and flexibility to respond to the multifarious global market demands, which are set in multicultural and intercultural contexts (Rockstuhl et al., 2011).

Cognitive cultural intelligence is a desirable trait for global market leaders. Ang and Van Dyne (2008) posited that individuals with high cognitive cultural intelligence are well-prepared decision-makers - armed with global market intelligence and able to respond through cross-cultural exchanges. Higher cognitive cultural intelligence supports a decision-maker's ability to acquire knowledge of different cultures from customs, economic systems, and social structures (Ang et al., 2007) to understanding cultural variances, recognizing how culture molds business practices, and ascertaining cultural values (Livermore, 2010). Higher cognitive cultural intelligence avails a strong platform for gathering global market information and processing this information into a compelling global market response.

Another conclusion from the study results is that a strong cognitive cultural intelligence has no direct bearing on how or if decision makers share global market information. A strong cognitive cultural intelligence will not propel the decision-maker to share any market information or any decided response with others. The sharing of global market information requires interpersonal and leadership skills, both of which are distinct from the cognitive component of cultural intelligence. Creque and Gooden (2011) contended that culturally intelligent leaders must have the necessary leadership and interpersonal skills to enhance the organization's ability to succeed in the global marketplace. Leaders must effect their own skills, aside from any cognitive cultural abilities, to share market information. Additionally, the sharing of market information takes time, effort, and organizational support. Kumar, Jones, Venkatesan, and Leone (2011) stated that the sharing of market customer and client information with peers in a company is a long-term performance approach in which the shared information adds to the collective organizational memory and supports the expansion of a learning organization. Other decision-makers, including leaders and peers, can use this collective, shared information to streamline their own global market approaches and raise their individual cognitive cultural intelligence.

Janssens's and Cappellen's (2008) study of cultural intelligence and global managers identified no significant link between cognitive cultural intelligence and global market strategic response, which differed from the current study findings showing a significant relationship. The authors suggested a potential reason was that the surveyed global managers admittedly spent so little time in the actual location due to short trips and air travel. Janssens and Cappellen's (2008) noted that participants felt that global market information acquisition was important and useful; however, the cognitive factors related to how this information was used were typically non-strategic, inconsistent, and often surprising. The current study findings are more likely to be true in situations where managers spend longer periods within other cultures or have longer and more substantial multi-cultural exchanges.

Metacognitive Cultural Intelligence and Global Market Orientation Factors

The study findings showed that metacognitive cultural intelligence had significant correlations to global market information acquisition and global market information sharing, while the findings showed no significant correlation to global market strategic response. From these findings, a conclusion is that a strong metacognitive cultural intelligence can be linked with how decision makers acquire and share global market information. A high metacognitive factor of cultural intelligence provides decision makers with enhanced thinking surrounding cultural interactions, experiences, and expectations (Klafehn, Banerjee, & Chiu, 2008). According to Kim and VanDyne (2012), metacognitive abilities enable decision makers to think about intercultural interactions before and after the occurrence. This deeper and more flexible thinking about cultural situations assists decision makers in evaluating multicultural exchanges within global markets, obtaining information about clients and customers, and sharing attained information.

Heightened metacognitive cultural intelligence promotes attention to the attainment of cultural knowledge and the relevance of a peer-aligned approach to global markets. Janssens and Cappellen (2008) suggested that global leaders understand the importance of the metacognition related to cultural situations, particularly to support awareness of cultural differences within markets. Successful global leaders recognize the importance of market approach alignment through communication among peers, encouraging a collective global market front rather than having each individual approaching the market in a different way (Janssens & Cappellen, 2008). The metacognitive cultural factor, which involves deeper awareness of cultural interactions (Rockstuhl et al., 2011), complements the sharing of global market information and cultural understandings among decision makers to build a shared understanding about the market and form a collective approach to that market.

Individuals who have higher metacognitive cultural intelligence and exhibit market-oriented behaviors are undoubtedly assets to their organizations and serve as global barometers. Globally-oriented leaders have a dynamic understanding of the international marketplace, are hyper-aware of multicultural exchanges, and can easily identify changes in different global markets (Monferrer, Blesa, & Ripollés, 2012). According to Klafehn, Banerjee, and Chiu (2008) and reinforced by Livermore (2010), this global-oriented hyper-awareness broadens a leader's viewpoint, decisions, and openness to new experiences, while giving perspective to how market data is acquired, analyzed, and used. Chua, Morris, and Mor (2012) added that metacognitive cultural leaders transform acquired market data and cultural experiences into creative collaborations and predictive strategies. Monferrer, Blesa, and Ripollés (2012) stated that global market-oriented behaviors are pivotal in obtaining international market intelligence and accelerating how organizational decision makers share this market intelligence to add to their organization's internal knowledgebase. Summarily, metacognitive cultural intelligence enables decision makers to think beyond their individual global experiences to creatively acquire market data, analyze the information, make projections based on that data, and incorporate the analysis into the collective market intellectual canon.

Another conclusion from the study results is that a decision maker's metacognitive cultural intelligence will not directly affect the global market strategic response. This result is surprising given that a strategic response is typically a well-thought out approach. However, since global market information acquisition and sharing with metacognitive cultural intelligence avails a collective, consensual approach to a global market (Janssens & Cappellen, 2008), strategic responses formed from such higher-level thinking may have more potency as a collective effort rather than an individual one.

Motivational Cultural Intelligence and Global Market Orientation Factors

The study findings, confirmed by literature, indicated that motivational cultural intelligence has significant correlation to only one global market orientation factor: global market information acquisition. The findings showed no significant correlation to global market information sharing or strategic response. An individual's cultural drive (Livermore, 2011; 2010), which makes up the motivational factor to cultural intelligence, is an individual's capacity and motivation to use cultural knowledge and experiences to develop a germane response (Early & Ang, 2003; Janssens & Cappellen, 2008; Livermore, 2011; 2010). A conclusion to the current study is that a connection existed between a decision maker's drive toward certain global markets, such as the engineering market used in the study, and the global data that was accessible by the individual, whether through personal cultural exchanges, learned information, organizational memory repositories, or peer-to-peer shared data.

Based on the findings, a significant relationship exists between the motivational factor and individual cultural information gathering and comprehension. Additionally based on the findings, the motivational factor holds no significance to the magnitude of the individual's efficiency or willingness in sharing cultural knowledge or developing responses based on that knowledge. Rockstahl et al. (2010) confirmed that motivational cultural intelligence avails an individual the capacity and drive to learn about different cultures and multi-cultural situations. Livermore (2010) added that the motivation factor is more about learning and adapting to cultural situations or global markets than sharing information or creating long-range strategies.

Expanding the current study findings, Livermore (2010) stated that some organizations try to train leaders on cross-cultural differences, but often fail because of reluctance to change, poor past cultural experiences, or a disinterest to learn. Leaders must be flexible and willing to experience new multi-cultural situations, learn about diverse customers or markets, and highlight individual competence. Kim and Van Dyne (2012), along with Templer, Tay, and Chandrasekar (2006), stated that leaders with high cultural intelligence are motivated to invest adequate time and energy to learning about global, culturally-diverse markets. Global market orientated leaders exhibit situational flexibility, awareness, proactiveness, and competence in diverse or new environments (Nummela, Saarenketo, & Puumalainen, 2004). Ultimately, the study's findings reflect that a decision maker's cultural drive is inward-focused, connected to the desire for new market and client information and less on how information can be transmitted or used.

Shokef and Erez's (2008) research differed from this study's finding related to motivational cultural intelligence. The authors derived that the motivational cultural intelligence factor had the strongest link to an individual's global identity and presence. Incidentally, the authors noted that individuals with high motivational cultural intelligence were more apt to be willing for participation in the global arena and ultimately led to specific behaviors and strategic actions. The current study did not reveal any significant relationships between motivational cultural intelligence and the global actions represented in the global market strategic response factor. However, there may be potential reasons for the difference. Shokef and Erez's (2008) study focused primarily on multi-cultural teams within an organization, whereas the current study focused on individuals within globally-focused organizations. This difference, however subtle, highlighted potential variances among the approaches of individuals working in a multicultural team with individuals focused solely on the multi-cultural market. Perhaps motivational cultural intelligence plays a heightened role in global market success when individuals work directly within a multi-cultural team atmosphere and a lesser role when individuals at domestic firms focus on the global multi-cultural marketplace.

Behavioral Cultural Intelligence and Global Market Orientation Factors

The behavioral factor of cultural intelligence proved the least connected to global market orientation. The study findings, confirmed by literature, revealed that behavioral market orientation had no significant relationship to how decision makers acquire, share, and respond to global market information. A conclusion from the study is that in the global engineering context, a decision maker's cultural knowledge or ability to share and use cultural information is a more demonstrated and measured characteristic than the ability to exhibit appropriate behaviors in multi-cultural environments. This conclusion does not undermine the importance of cultural behaviors, as stated by Livermore (2011; 2010) and Earley and Peterson (2004); however, the significance of behaviors may prove situational, particularly among multi-cultural teams as observed in Shokef and Erez's (2008) research, and less significant with senior decision-makers with functions similar to the study participants. By sharing and using cultural information, the decision maker has the opportunity to understand the target global market from a holistic perspective and garner other decision maker viewpoints. Engineering leaders base decisions on this holistic, multi-viewpoint approach and, as the findings revealed, resort less on demonstrations of appropriate behaviors for the targeted region.

Kim and Van Dyne (2012) differed from this study's findings, identifying a connection between cultural behaviors with prior experience responding to multi-cultural markets. They stated specifically that individuals with more prior multi-cultural experiences and a history of responding to multi-cultural needs should have the flexibility needed to exhibit appropriate verbal and non-verbal behaviors during diverse exchanges. Kim and Van Dyne (2012) added that prior experience responding to multi-cultural market demands and behavioral cultural intelligence are mutually complementary and related. The current study did not indicate any significant relationship between behavioral cultural intelligence and any element of global market orientation. Perhaps the current study findings differ from Kim and Van Dyne (2012) because the current study involves global engineering decision makers from globally-leading organizations, whereas Kim and Van Dyne's (2012) study focused largely on how the minority status of firms intervenes with cultural intelligence.

The behavioral elements of global leaders in cultural exchanges may be less understood than other dimensions. Rockstahl et al. (2011) took a different approach stating that cultural behaviors in global leaders focused on the intellectual starting at the brain's neurological level. They stated that the development of a global leader from multicultural, global exchanges is the product of acquired and changing cognitive habits before becoming a behavior. The findings of the current study indicated no significant relationship between behavioral cultural intelligence and the sub-factors of global market orientation. Since the study participants have documented global experience with measured cultural cognitive habits, there exists ambiguity between the Rockstahl et al. (2011) findings surrounding cultural behaviors and the current study findings. A possible reason for this disconnect could be insufficient levels of measurement for acquired behaviors in the current study instruments or unique characteristics of the global engineering market.

Not wholly disconnected from Rockstahl et al.'s (2011) findings, this study's results, particularly the resultant participant ages and length in the current role, support Rockstahl et al.'s (2011) findings that acquired habits lead to cultural behaviors. The 51-60 and over 80 age groups made up more than 70 percent of the global leader respondents. Those in their current decision-making role from 6-10 years and more than 20 years, comprised the largest percentages of global leader participants (31.58% and 21.05% respectively). Both characteristics indicate that those with more experience have had more time and opportunity to turn cognitive habits into behaviors. Surpassing any conclusions from this study and as indicated later in the chapter's recommendations, there exists a need for further research and understanding to gain a clearer understanding to the relationship between behavioral cultural intelligence and the factors of global market orientation.

Implications of the Study

The discoveries of this study provide insights into how the connection between cultural intelligence and global market orientation is important to engineering decision makers doing business globally. Chapter 1 detailed the importance of examining the relationships between the four factors of cultural intelligence and three factors of global market orientation on the individual level. The outcome of hypotheses testing of these factors along with the testing of aggregate values indicate that recognized global engineering decision makers possess and apply an amalgamation of cultural intelligence and global market orientation abilities. The study findings have implications for enhancing the global market success of U.S.-based engineering firms with regard to leadership practices, global market orientation approaches, and the cultural intelligence of staff.

Implications for Leadership

The study results support the importance of incorporating cultural intelligence and market orientation into global leader skillsets. A decision maker with international experience does not necessarily indicate that the decision maker is culturally competent or has the intimate understandings of how best to conduct business globally. Rockstuhl, Hong, Ng, Ang, and Chiu (2010) agreed that not all leaders with multicultural experiences are culturally capable or prepared for global exchanges. However, there exists empirical evidence that cultural and global market skills can be developed or enhanced over time through training, expatriation and personal leadership development (Boyacigiller, 1991; Kim & Van Dyne, 2012; Livermore, 2011, 2010; Ng, Van Dyne, & Ang, 2009). As with other leadership skills and irrespective of having international experience, decision makers can develop or refine cultural and global leadership through training.

The study results imply the importance of leadership realignment from domestically-driven leadership into dynamic, location-nonspecific leadership through the measured relationships of cognitive cultural intelligence to global market strategic response, and metacognitive cultural intelligence to global market information sharing. The U.S.-based study participants have acknowledged global success in part by realigning their domestic approaches to the border-spanning global market. Domestic and global markets are significantly different (Alimienė & Kuvykaitė, 2008; Valenti, 1995) and require globally-aimed leaders to realign, and in some cases migrate from, their domestic approach to a more universal and dynamic approach. Individual cultural intelligence and market orientation factors play potent roles in this leadership realignment. Culturally intelligent leaders who have satisfactory leadership and interpersonal skills will enhance the organization's ability to penetrate and succeed in the global marketplace (Creque & Gooden, 2011). The study findings indicated that the cognitive and metacognitive cultural abilities of leaders have significant links to the acquisition, sharing, and implementation of global market information in the worldwide marketplace. These cultural and marketplace skills are not associated with any one location, be it domestic or international, but are rather location-non-specific skills. Supported by the participant's global engineering market successes, the study findings imply that culturally intelligent leaders need to go beyond thinking and responding as they would domestically or within a single location, and transform their leadership approaches to support an *any location* approach.

The findings indicate relationships between a leader's global market strategic response and how that individual thinks about the market and exhibits cultural intelligent cognitive habits. These findings imply the need for global managers to build their global approaches around experienced cultural exchanges and acquired cultural knowledge. The findings also indicated that the strategic thinking of culturally-aware global leaders (metacognitive cultural intelligence) is related to how they learn and share global knowledge, namely global market information acquisition and sharing. These findings imply the necessity for a focused process by which leaders go beyond just knowledge acquisition into strategically analyzing multi-cultural environments, exchanges, and situations, and sharing their understandings. The overall implication is the ability to transform individual cultural knowledge and experience into a repository for peer-to-peer sharing and growth.

For success, leaders need to embrace and learn about new cultural and global markets. Kim and Van Dyne (2012) predicted that leaders with high cultural and market competency would be viewed by others as being better suited to meet the needs of and lead complex international assignments. As target business moves from domestic markets to global ones, once domestically driven leaders face the challenge of managing diverse, multi-cultural teams (Rockstuhl et al., 2010). Leadership realignment, in addition to training and further development, is important for cultural awareness and global leadership prowess.

Implications to Cultural Intelligence

The findings from the study have implications for use of the aggregate and sub-factors of cultural intelligence by leaders, decision-makers, team management, and for staff hiring and development. Acquiring information involves cognitive and often metacognitive processes, and, as validated by Earley and Peterson (2004), can be accomplished for cultural intelligence through targeted training by an experienced individual and systematic measurement of global staff through the use of validated instruments such as Earley and Peterson's (2004) Cultural Intelligence Scale. As the findings indicate, the cognitive and metacognitive factors of cultural intelligence relate significantly to the acquisition of global market information. Determining a staff member's individual cultural intelligence score can facilitate targeted cultural training followed by further cultural intelligence measurement for improvement evaluation.

An implication of the study's findings is that decision makers might benefit from the migration and use of cultural intelligence measurement and training as keystones to their global business approach. Individuals with mature cultural skills can have positive impact on the organization's overall global and fiscal performance. Bucher (2008) suggested cultural intelligence stems from individual leaders and spreads throughout the organization, influencing organizational success, productivity, client relationships, and operational existence in the marketplace. Livermore (2011; 2010), a strong supporter of training, suggested that cultural intelligence training should be a part of every leader's development plan. The use of cross-cultural testing and analysis of individual leaders, such as the CQS instrument and psychological tests, can help identify training areas to stimulate staff development, organizational improvement, and process changes (Matsumoto & Hwang, 2013). As stated earlier, the use of the CQS in tandem with targeted training can help develop individuals into more culturally aware leaders and measure their individual progress before and after cultural training. Individual and organizational promotion of cultural intelligence development might have a positive ripple effect on transforming the organizational culture, nurturing better global leaders and decision makers, and the selection of markets.

The study's findings have other implications that pertain to the cultural intelligence subfactors. Less than half (41.67%) of the cultural intelligence subfactors were significantly related to global market orientation subfactors; however, the aggregate variables are significantly related. This implies that global leaders do not need to possess competency in all cultural intelligence subfactors for successful global market prowess. The findings also signify that certain subfactors may hold stronger connections to global proficiency than others, such as cultural intelligence cognition and metacognition.

The behavioral cultural intelligence subfactor has no significant relationships to any global market orientation subfactor. This finding implies that cultural behaviors may have lesser importance in global engineering marketplace approaches than the other subfactors. This implication contrasts with Kim and Van Dyne (2012), who stated that individuals experienced in multi-cultural situations, analogous to the study's participants, should have the flexibility needed to exhibit appropriate behaviors during multi-cultural interactions. As addressed in the study recommendations section, the findings involving behavioral cultural intelligence imply the need for a larger sample population to deliver improved and more convincing results.

Limitations

The small number of willing participants posed a potential limitation to the study. The study involved 38 voluntary participants; however, invited participants comprised over 900 global decision makers from ENR-listed firms. Although the study was credible, generalizable, and met reliable correlational study requirements (Gay, Mills, & Airasian, 2011), the small response may limit the breadth of the results. Likewise, the exclusion of potential data from non-participating decision makers poses a threat to the statistical validity of the findings.

A second limitation of the study involves the generalizability of the results. The study results have roots with U.S.-based firms and may not be generalizable to decision makers from non-U.S. engineering firms. Participants in the research were all executive and influential engineering and marketing decision makers from the top U.S.-based globalized engineering firms. The results may have domestic bias that may not be useable at Non-U.S.-based firms. Similarly, a possible limitation exists regarding the results, which are from ENR-listed, top U.S.-based globalized engineering firms. The results may not be relatable to some smaller, less globalized domestic engineering firms, such as engineering firms classified as a Small Business Enterprise. Likewise, these study results also may not be relatable to some engineering domestic Minority-Owned Business and Women-Owned Business Enterprises.

Participant diversity may be a possible limitation to the study. Although the engineering industry has traditionally been a male-dominated field, male participants still outnumbered female participants two-thirds to one-third resulting in a potential over-representation of males compared to the population. Additionally, participants with Non-Hispanic/Latino ethnic backgrounds overwhelmingly outnumbered Hispanic/Latino participants (Non-Hispanic/Latino = 97.37%) resulting in a possible over-representation of Non-Hispanic ethnicities compared to the population. Similarly, participants with a race defined as White/Caucasian/European (86.84%) outnumbered the various other race categories in this study. No participants were Middle Eastern and Pacific Islander and resulted in a possible under-representation of these races.

Another potential limitation is sample bias. Some ENR-listed, top U.S.-based globalized engineering firms had multiple decision makers participate in the study, while others had only one participant and others had no voluntary representation. Because the study involved a differing number of participants from each organization due to participant availability, random selection, and choice, the differing level of organizational participation might pose a risk of sample bias.

A final potential limitation to the study involves the different participant approaches toward the points on the Likert-type scale, including interpretation, response style, and use of the scale (Church & Waclawski, 1998; Neuman, 2006). Respondents come from different ethnic backgrounds and possess individually different experiences. As such, different respondents might interpret, respond, and use the study's scale differently. Variations in response styles and scale usage may pose limitations to the study findings.

Recommendations for Future Research and Practice

A need for further research regarding the correlation between cultural intelligence and global market orientation may exist. Similarly, a need may also exist for future implementation of both concepts, cultural intelligence and global market orientation, into general business practices. Recommendations to support these purported needs follow, classified among future research recommendations and practice recommendations.

Future Research Recommendations

One research recommendation is for future researchers to reproduce this study using a larger sample size from the same population of ENR listed top global and international firms. A larger sample size would provide depth in the results due to analysis with a higher confidence level and smaller confidence interval. A larger sample size might also illuminate the relationship between past global experiences and behavioral cultural intelligence with the factors of global market orientation. Faherty (2008) concurred that a larger sample size allows the researcher to obtain a truer representation of the studied population. A recommendation is to heighten outreach and enlistment of participants for a larger sample size. Specific outreach to and cooperation with the executive level of large global engineering companies on the ENR list may support the necessary enlistment of participants.

Another recommendation for further research is to replicate this study using an expanded population – a population that transcends the ENR listed firms. This expanded population could include the top global engineering firms with smaller engineering concerns that have some degree of overseas business but not enough to make the ENR ranked lists. The expanded population would also allow for a wider spectrum of viewpoints from decision makers well placed in the global market to those who have irregular or niche footholds in the global marketplace. A variation of this future research recommendation would be to include all of the top global firms on the ENR list, regardless of the firm's base country. Including all top firms would inject a more globalized viewpoint to the results with a population not solely with American idealisms or interests. The expanded study would have results with implications worldwide rather than just in the United States.

Another possibility for further research is to replicate this study with a global industry other than engineering. Alternate industries that have a global reach may include healthcare, education, real estate, and manufacturing. An alternate industry would require a different population and may illustrate different ways market orientation and cultural intelligence are applied in global decision making. Similarly, it would be interesting to research a specific type of engineering rather than engineering as a composite. Some of the major global engineering disciplines include electrical, civil/structural, mechanical, power, environmental, and biomedical engineering. For this type of focused study, it may be prudent to fine-tune the current population with coordination with a predominant professional engineering society for the specific discipline. For example, the Institute for Electrical and Electronic Engineers (IEEE) association would be the best source to identify specific global electrical engineers.

Another recommendation for further research is to conduct a qualitative study to explore how decision-makers use cultural intelligence and global market orientation in their current leadership roles. This type of study could clarify or give perspective to why some of the current study's relationships were found significant and others not. Cooper and Schindler (2003) acknowledged the use of a qualitative research method for the exploration of variable relationships and characteristics. Differing from the current study, a qualitative study could offer findings at a more exacting level and bare leadership patterns for modeling and practice. Similarly, another interesting qualitative research project would be to conduct a grounded theory study of the process for integrating cultural intelligence, global market orientation, and their sub-elements into existing leadership approaches. A grounded theory study could potentially expose whether one variable is a practical predecessor to the other or whether they develop simultaneously. This grounded theory study could also explore predecessor relationships between the multiple variable sub-elements.

The study's findings indicated the insignificant relationships behavioral cultural intelligence has with the three subfactors of global market orientation. A further research recommendation is to conduct a study that focuses specifically on how behavioral cultural intelligence relates to the global market orientation factors. The study could survey leaders on specific cultural behaviors related to the global marketplace and clientele. Perhaps the target industry could span outside of engineering into other professional fields, such as medicine, finance, or manufacturing.

The last recommendation for further research is to conduct the study with a focus on specific organizational structures rather than a specific industry or global ranking. The current study did not impose limitations on organizational structures. Subsequently, the current study gave no bearing to how a global decision maker's market orientation and cultural intelligence relates to their organizational structures. However, it would be interesting to research if different organizational structures, such as functional, divisional, and matrix structures, influence or align the cultural malleability and market understanding of their global decision makers.

Practice Recommendations

A recommendation for actionable practice involves the use of the CQS for personal leadership development. According to Livermore (2010), cultural intelligence is far more than a leader's knowledge of cultural differences, but rather encompasses a leader's individual interests, global-based strategies, cultural thinking, and behaviors. Since the CQS is a validated measure of an individual's cultural intelligence, the results can identify personal strengths and weaknesses related to cultural intelligence behaviors, motivation, cognitive and meta-cognitive. These results can help identify personal improvement pathways and provide revised focal points to an individual's personal leadership development plan.

The CQS can also distinguish the need for further cultural engagements to support personal and global leadership development. Rockstuhl et al. (2010) suggested that a global leader's personal development flourishes with every cultural engagement because, through repeat exposure, the leader can obtain the cognitive habits necessary to meet the expectations of different cultures. The CQS results can expose those areas requiring deeper development and bolster the mindfulness and self-awareness necessary for personal leadership growth.

Although leveraging cross-cultural or multi-cultural environments can enhance a leader's personal development, leaders can also benefit and grow from understanding how well they learn from these cultural experiences. Ng, Van Dyne, and Ang (2009) acknowledged that not all individuals have the ability to learn from and leverage their cross-cultural or multi-cultural experiences. The CQS can help determine a leader's level of cultural learning ability through comparing an individual's initial answers with responses from a second CQS taken after a period of increased exposure to multi-cultural situations. Once again, this before and after analysis of the results could help refine an individual's personal global leadership growth plan and identify areas requiring deeper focus.

A further recommendation is to use the CQS to evaluate employee needs and begin targeted training of globally-focused staff to the principles of cultural intelligence. The results would help management determine an employee's cross-cultural baseline and evaluate that employee's cultural abilities with respect to the collective employee population. The information gathered from the CQS can have practical implications for developing employees into global leaders. Management could also explore the possibilities of integrating cultural intelligence training into the standard portfolio of employee development programs.

For those leaders targeting the global market, another practice recommendation is to develop location nonspecific leadership. Culturally intelligent leaders can work across cultural and international borders seamlessly and are not associated with any one location (Livermore, 2011; Livermore, 2010). Leaders should be flexible in their approach and build individual awareness for different cultures, work approaches, and target market particulars. Livermore (2010) suggested the importance for leaders to remain flexible and culturally aware to facilitate the appropriate leadership style in any situation or location. This leadership trait can improve an individual's ability (and their organization's ability) to penetrate and succeed in the global marketplace.

During employee onboarding, the CQS can be used to avail management the ability to hire professionals who are not only technically competent, but interculturally savvy as well. Ng, Van Dyne, and Ang (2009) suggested that cultural intelligence could serve as an employee selection tool to enhance staff learning and strengthen the relationship between experience and effectiveness for employees with international responsibilities. Understanding the benefits of existing and potential employee cross-cultural experiences can support the development of effective project teams and meaningful new employee hires.

Since the global market information acquisition subfactor had the most significant relationships with the cultural intelligence subfactors, a practice recommendation is for leaders to afford more focused effort on receiving global market intelligence and on the dynamics of that data. More astute efforts during the data acquisition phase of their global market strategy might be an efficient use of their time and provide positive global market results.

A final practice recommendation is to use the I-MARKOR to evaluate an employee's understanding of the overseas marketplace and to acknowledge where individual global market strengths lie. With a focus on global markets, the I-MARKOR can be used to measure how an employee acquires, shares, and responds to global market information while exposing the varying ways market-oriented behaviors are used in the company to attract new work (Schlosser & McNaughton, 2009). Holistically, an organization's management can use the data gathered from the I-MARKOR as an amalgamated snapshot of the company's highly used and underused market orientation best practices. As Bell and Kozlowski (2002) stated, employee market-oriented behaviors provide the essential data necessary for the firm's overall success in a market. Individually, an organization's management can use the data gathered from each I-MARKOR to distinguish the areas of strength, areas where the employee can serve as a mentor to others, and the areas of needed growth, areas where the employee can benefit from mentored development. The I-MARKOR can be a singular tool to help organizational management review their staffing approach, readdress their business objectives, and revise their global mission.

Conclusion

Chapter 5 included an interpretation of the collected data and study findings. Although a significant relationship existed between aggregate cultural intelligence and aggregate global market orientation, each cultural intelligence factor was evaluated with the global market orientation dimensions. The results indicated that a strong cognitive cultural intelligence can be associated with how decision makers acquire and respond to global market information, but has no direct bearing on how or if decision makers share global market information. A strong cognitive cultural intelligence will not propel the decision-maker to share any market information or any decided response with others.

The findings indicated that a strong metacognitive cultural intelligence can have a positive effect on how decision makers acquire and share global market information, but will not directly affect the global market strategic response. A high metacognitive factor of cultural intelligence provides decision makers with higher-level thinking surrounding cultural interactions, experiences, and expectations. Monferrer, Blesa, and Ripollés (2012) supported this finding stating that global market-oriented behaviors are pivotal in obtaining international market intelligence and accelerating how organizational decision makers share this market intelligence to add to their organization's internal knowledgebase.

The study demonstrated a connection between a decision maker's motivation toward certain global markets and the global data that is accessible by the individual, whether through personal cultural exchanges, learned information, organizational memory repositories, or peer-to-peer shared data. Supporting these findings, Livermore (2010) stated that the motivation factor is more about learning and adapting to cultural situations or global markets than about sharing information or creating long-range strategies. The findings indicated that a decision maker's cultural drive is inward-focused, connected to the desire for new market and client information and less on how information can be shared or used.

The results also revealed that the behavioral factor of cultural intelligence was the least related to the factors of global market orientation. In the global engineering context, a decision maker's ability to exhibit appropriate behaviors and exchanges in multi-cultural environments is passive to that decision maker's cultural knowledge or ability to use cultural information. Contrary to the results, Kim and Van Dyne (2012) and Gelfand, Imai, and Fehr (2008) suggested prior intercultural experiences and global exchanges develop cultural behaviors.

The study findings may have implications for leadership, global market orientation, and cultural intelligence. One implication may be that decision makers can develop or refine cultural and global leadership through training. The findings from the study indicated the importance of leadership realignment from domestically-driven leadership into dynamic, location-nonspecific leadership. This leadership realignment, in addition to training and individual development, is important for cultural awareness, increased flexibility, and global leadership prowess. Another implication of the study may be the necessity of cultural training and testing. As Matsumoto and Hwang (2013) stated, cross-cultural testing and analysis of individual leaders help identify training areas to stimulate staff development, organizational improvement, and process changes.

The limitations of the study included the small number of willing participants, the generalizability of the results, participant diversity, and participant approaches to the different participant approaches toward the points on the Likert-type scale instruments. The small response may have limited the breadth of the results, as well as the high amount of participants with Non-Hispanic/Latino ethnic backgrounds. Finally, because the study involved a differing number of participants from each organization due to participant availability, random selection, and choice, the differing level of organizational participation may pose a risk of sample bias.

This chapter presented recommendations for future research and practice. One research recommendation was for future researchers to reproduce this study using a larger sample size from the same population of ENR listed top global and international firms. A second recommendation for future research was to replicate this study using an expanded population that is beyond the ENR listed firms. A last recommendation for future research suggested possibility for further research is to replicate this study with a global industry other than engineering, such as healthcare, education, real estate, and manufacturing.

A first recommendation for actionable practice involved the use of the CQS for proactive personal leadership development. The CQS can be used to determine the need for further cultural engagements, which can support personal and global leadership development. Another practice recommendation was to use the CQS to evaluate employee needs and begin targeted training of globally focused staff to the principles of cultural intelligence. The final practice recommendation was to use the I-MARKOR to evaluate an employee's understanding of the overseas marketplace and to acknowledge where individual global market strengths lie. Use of the CQS and I-MARKOR instruments, and other similar scales, can enhance onboarding activities to identify culturally competent new hires.

REFERENCES

Acosta, C., Leon, V. J., Conrad, C., & Malave, C. O. (2010). *Global engineering: Design, decision making, and communication.* Boca Raton, FL: CRC Press.

Alexander, J., & Wilson, M. S. (1997). Leading across cultures: Five vital capabilities. In F. Hesselbein, M. Goldsmith, & R. Beckhard. (Eds). *The organization of the future* (pp. 287-294). San Francisco: Jossey-Bass.

Alimienė, M., & Kuvykaitė, R. (2008). Standardization/adaptation of marketing solutions in companies operating in foreign markets: An integrated approach. *Engineering Economics, 56*(1), 37-47. Retrieved from http://internet.ktu.lt/lt/mokslas/zurnalai/inzeko/56/1392-2758-2008-1-56-37.pdf

American Council of Engineering Companies. (2013). *About ACEC.* Retrieved from http://www.acec.org/about/index.cfm

American Marketing Association. (2007). Definition of Marketing. Retrieved from http://www.marketingpower.com/AboutAMA/Pages/DefinitionofMarketing.aspx

Amiri, A., Moghimi, S., & Kazemi, M. (2010). Studying the Relationship between Cultural Intelligence and Employees' Performance. *European Journal of Scientific Research, 42*(3), 418-427. Retrieved from http://www.europeanjournalofscientificresearch.com/

Ang, S., & Inkpen, A. C. (2008). Cultural Intelligence and Offshore Outsourcing Success: A Framework of Firm-Level Intercultural Capability. *Decision Sciences, 39*(3), 337-358. doi:10.1111/j.1540-5915.2008.00195.x

Ang, S., & Van Dyne, L. (2008). Conceptualization of cultural intelligence: Definition, distinctiveness, and nomological network. In S. Ang, & L. Van Dyne (Eds.), *Handbook of cultural intelligence: Theory, measurement, and applications* (pp. 3-15). Armonk, NY: M. E. Sharpe.

Ang, S., Van Dyne, L., & Koh, C. (2006). Personality correlates of the four-factor model of cultural intelligence. *Group and Organization Management, 31*(1), 100-123. doi: 10.1177/1059601105275267

Ang, S., Van Dyne, L., Koh, C., Ng, K. Y., Templer, K. J., Tay, C., & Chandrasekar, N. A. (2007). Cultural intelligence: Its measurement and effects on cultural judgment and decision making, cultural adaptation and task performance. *Management and Organization Review, 3*(3), 335–371. doi: 10.1111/j.1740-8784.2007.00082.x

Behi, R., & Nolan, M. (1996). Causality and control: threats to internal validity. *British Journal of Nursing (Mark Allen Publishing), 5*(6), 374-377. Retrieved from http://www.britishjournalofnursing.com/

Bell, B. S., & Kozlowski, S. W. J. (2002). Goal orientation and ability: Interactive effects on self-efficacy, performance and knowledge. *Journal of Applied Psychology, 87*(3): 497-505. doi: 10.1037/0021-9010.87.3.497

Berry, J. W. (1974). Radical cultural relativism and the concept of intelligence. In J. W. Berry & P. R. Dasen (Eds.), *Culture and cognition: readings in cross cultural psychology* (pp. 225-229). London, U.K.: Methuen.

Boyacigiller, N. (1991). The international assignment reconsidered. In M. Mendenhall and G. Oddou (Eds.), *Readings and Cases in International Human Resource Management* (pp. 148-155). Boston: PWS Kent.

Brettel, M., Engelen, A., Heinemann, F., & Vadhanasindhu, P. (2008). Antecedents of market orientation: A cross-cultural comparison. *Journal of International Marketing, 16*(2), 84-119. doi:10.1509/jimk.16.2.84

Brown, A. S. (2009). A shift in engineering offshore. *Mechanical Engineering, 131*(3), 24-29. Retrieved from http://www.asme.org/products/journals/mechanical-engineering

Bucher, R. D. (2008). *Building cultural intelligence (CQ): Nine megaskills*. Upper Saddle River, NJ: Pearson Prentice Hall.

Buckley, B. (2010, December). Global expansions yield opportunities for firms: With fierce competition, firms diversify and make acquisitions. *Engineering News Record, 265*(17), p. 47-48. Retrieved from ENR.com.

Bueno, C. M., & Tubbs, S. L. (2004). Identifying Global Leadership Competencies: An Exploratory Study. *Journal of American Academy of Business, Cambridge, 5*(1/2), 80-87. Retrieved from http://www.jaabc.com/journal.htm

Cadogan, J. W., Kuivalainen, O., & Sundqvist, S. (2009). Export Market-Oriented Behavior and Export Performance: Quadratic and Moderating Effects Under Differing Degrees of Market Dynamism and Internationalization. *Journal of International Marketing, 17*(4), 71-89. doi: 10.1509/jimk.17.4.71

Campbell, D. T., & Stanley, J. C. (1963). *Experimental and quasi-experimental designs for research*. Chicago, IL: Rand McNally.

Cano, C. R., Carrillat, F. A., & Jaramillo, F. (2004). A meta-analysis of the relationship between market orientation and business performance: evidence from five continents. *International Journal of Research in Marketing, 21*(2), 179-200. doi: 10.1016/j.ijresmar.2003.07.001

Cayla, J., & Arnould, E. J. (2008). A Cultural Approach to Branding in the Global Marketplace. *Journal of International Marketing, 16*(4), 86-112. doi: 10.1509/jimk.16.4.86

Ceyhan, K. (2004). An investigation of the antecedents and consequences of individual-level customer orientation: A comprehensive approach. (Doctoral dissertation). Available from ProQuest Dissertations and Theses database. (UMI No. 3163526)

Chaney, L. H., & Martin, J. S. (2006). Global business customs and etiquette. *OfficePro, 66*(4), 18. Retrieved from http://www.iaap-hq.org/publications/officepro

Chen, P. Y., & Popovich, P. M. (2002). *Correlation: Parametric and nonparametric measures.* Sage Publishers: Thousand Oaks, CA.

Chua, R. Y. J., Morris, M. W., & Mor, S. (2012). *Collaborating across cultures: Cultural metacognition & affect-based trust in creative collaboration.* Rochester: Social Science Research Network. doi:http://dx.doi.org/10.2139/ssrn.1861054

Church, A. H., & Waclawski, J. (1998). *Designing and using organizational surveys: A seven-step process.* San Francisco, CA: Jossey-Bass.

Cobley, P. (2004). Marketing the 'glocal' in narratives of national identity. *Semiotica,* 150(1-4), 197-225. doi: 10.1515/semi.2004.043

Cook, T. D., & Campbell, D. T. (1979). *Quasi-experimentation: design and analysis issues for field settings.* Chicago, IL: Rand McNally.

Cooper, D. R., & Schindler, P. S. (2003). Business research methods. (8th ed.).New York, NY: McGraw-Hill Companies.

Creque, C. A., & Gooden, D. J. (2011). Cultural intelligence and global business competencies: A framework for organizational effectiveness in the global marketplace. *International Journal of Management and Information Systems;* Fourth Quarter 2011; 15(4). Retrieved from http://journals.cluteonline.com/index.php/IJMIS/article/view/5812

Culbert, K. (2011, March). IBISWorld Industry Report 54133: Engineering Services in the US. [Electronic version]. *IBISWorld.* Retrieved from http://www.ibisworld.com/

Cultural Intelligence Center. (2005). The 20-item four factor CQS (the CQ Scale). Retrieved at http://www.culturalq.com/docs/The%20CQS.pdf

Dean, B. P. (2007). Cultural intelligence in global leadership: A model for developing culturally and nationally diverse teams (Doctoral dissertation). Available from ProQuest Dissertations and Theses database. (UMI No. 3292256)

de la Garza-Carranza, M., & Egri, C. P. (2010). Managerial cultural intelligence and small business in Canada. *Management Revue, 21*(3), 353-371. doi:10.1688/1861-9908_mrev_2010_03_de-la-Garza-Carranza

de Mooij, M. (2010). *Global marketing and advertising: Understanding cultural paradoxes*. (3rd ed.). Los Angeles, CA: Sage Publications.

Deng, S., & Dart, J. (1994). Measuring market orientation: A Multi-factor, multi-item approach. *Journal of Marketing Management, 10*(8), 725-742. doi: 10.1080/0267257X.1994.9964318

Deshpandé, R., & Farley, J. U. (1998). Measuring market orientation: generalization and synthesis. *Journal of Market-Focused Management, 2*(3), 213-232, doi: 10.1023/A:1009719615327

Deshpandé, R., Farley, J. U., & Webster Jr., F. E. (1993). Corporate culture customer orientation, and innovativeness in Japanese firms: A quadrad analysis. *Journal of Marketing, 57*(1), 23-37. Retrieved from http://www.jstor.org/discover/10.2307/1252055?uid=3739712&uid=2134&uid=2&uid=70&uid=4&uid=3739256&sid=21102049236967

Diamantopoulos, A., & Cadogan, J. W. (1996). Internationalizing the market orientation construction: An in-depth interview approach. *Journal of Strategic Marketing, 4*(1), 23-52. doi: 10.1080/09652549600000002

Drucker, P. F. (1997). Introduction: Toward the new organization. In F. Hesselbein, M. Goldsmith, & R. Beckhard. (Eds). *The organization of the future* (pp. 1-5). San Francisco: Jossey-Bass.

Earley, P. C., & Ang, S. (2003). *Cultural intelligence: Individual interactions across cultures*. Stanford, CA: Stanford University Press.

Earley, P., & Peterson, R. S. (2004). The elusive cultural chameleon: Cultural intelligence as a new approach to intercultural training for the global manager. *Academy Of Management Learning & Education, 3*(1), 100-115. doi:10.5465/AMLE.2004.12436826

Elenkov, D. S., & Pimentel, J. R. C. (2008). Social intelligence, emotional intelligence, and cultural intelligence: An integrative perspective. In S. Ang, & L. Van Dyne (Eds.), *Handbook of cultural intelligence: Theory, measurement, and applications* (pp. 289-305). Armonk, NY: M. E. Sharpe.

Eysenck, H. J. (1986). A theory of intelligence and the psychophysiology of cognition. In R. J. Sternberg (Ed.), *Advances in the psychology of human intelligence* (Vol. 3, pp. 1-34). Hillsdale, NJ: Erlbaum.

Faherty, V. E. (2008). *Compassionate statistics: Applies quantitative analysis for social services (with exercises and instructions for SPSS)*. Thousand Oaks, CA: Sage Publications.

Farrell, M., & Oczkowski, E. (1998). An analysis of the MKTOR and MARKOR measures of market orientation: An Australian perspective. *Marketing Bulletin, 8*, 30-40. Retrieved from http://marketing-bulletin.massey.ac.nz/V8/MB_V8_A3_Farrell.pdf

Felton, A. P. (1959). Making the marketing concept work. *Harvard Business*

Review, 37(4), 55-65. Retrieved from http://hbr.org/magazine

Ferguson, J. L., Dadzie, K. Q., & Johnston, W. J. (2008). Country-of-origin effects in service evaluation in emerging markets: some insights from five West African countries. *The Journal of Business & Industrial Marketing, 23*(6), 429-437. doi: 10.1108/08858620810894472

Fuller, B. (2004, March). Offshoring has hit home. *Electronic Engineering Times*, (1314), 84. Retrieved from http://www.eetimes.com/

Fung, V. K., Fung, W. K., & Wind, Y. (2008). *Competing in a flat world: Building enterprise for a borderless world*. Upper Saddle River, NJ: Pearson Education.

Gardner, H. (1983) *Frames of Mind: The theory of multiple intelligences*, New York: Basic Books.

Gardner, H. (1993). *Multiple intelligence: The theory in practice*. New York: Basic Books.

Gardner, H. (2006). *Multiple intelligences: New horizons*. New York: Basic Books.

Gauzente, C. (1999). Comparing market orientation scales: A content analysis. *Marketing Bulletin, 10*, 76-82. Retrieved from http://marketing-bulletin.massey.ac.nz/V10/MB_V10_N4_Gauzente.pdf

Gay, L. R., Mills, G. E., & Airasian, P. W. (2011). *Educational research: Competencies for analysis and applications*. (10th ed.). Pearson: Upper Saddle River, NJ.

Gelfand, M. J., Imai, L., & Fehr, R. (2008). Thinking intelligently about cultural intelligence: The road ahead. In S. Ang, & L. Van Dyne (Eds.), *Handbook of cultural intelligence: Theory, measurement, and applications* (pp. 375-387). Armonk, NY: M. E. Sharpe.

Gertsen, M. C. (1990). Intercultural competence and expatriates, *International Journal of Human Resources Management, 1*(3), 341–362. do

Hadcroft, P., & Jarratt, D. (2007). Market orientation: An iterative process of customer and market engagement. *Journal of Business-to-Business Marketing, 14*(3), 21-57. doi: 10.1300/J033v14n03_02

Hansen, J. D., Tanuja, S., Weilbaker, D. C., & Guesalaga, R. (2011). Cultural intelligence in cross-cultural selling: Propositions and directions for future research. *Journal of Personal Selling & Sales Management, 31*(3), 243-254. doi: 10.2753/PSS0885-3134310303

Ho, V. B., Niden, P., & Johneny, S. (2011). Market orientation of individuals: A study on the remisiers in Malaysia. Proceedings of the Annual Summit on Business and Entrepreneurial Studies, Malaysia, 387-395. Retrieved from http://www.internationalconference.com.my/proceeding/asbes2011_proceeding/030_187_ASBES2011_Proceeding_PG0387_0395.pdf

Hofstede, G. (1980). *Culture's consequences: International differences in work-related values*. Beverly Hills, CA: Sage Publications.

Hofstede, G., & Hofstede, G. J. (2005). Cultures and organizations: Software of the mind. (2nd ed.). New York, NY: McGraw-Hill Companies.

House, R. J., Hanges, P. J., Javidan, M., Dorfman, P. W., & Gupta, V. (2004). *Culture, leadership, and organizations: The GLOBE study of 62 societies*. Thousand Oaks, CA: Sage.

Hult, G. T. M, Snow, C. C., & Kandemir, D. (2003). The role of entrepreneurship in building cultural competitiveness in different organizational types. *Journal of Management, 29*(3), 401-426. doi: 10.1016/S0149-2063_03_00017-5

IBISWorld Inc. (2009, April). IBISWorld Industry Report: Engineering Services in the US: 54133. Retrieved from http://www.ibisworld.com/

IBISWorld Inc. (2010, September). IBISWorld Industry Report: Global Engineering Services: L6722-GL. Retrieved from http://www.ibisworld.com/

IBISWorld Inc. (2012, July). IBISWorld Industry Report: Global Engineering Services: L6722-GL. Retrieved from http://www.ibisworld.com/

Janssens, M., & Cappellen, T. (2008). Contextualizing cultural intelligence: The case of global managers. In S. Ang, & L. Van Dyne (Eds.), *Handbook of cultural intelligence: Theory, measurement, and applications* (pp. 356-371). Armonk, NY: M. E. Sharpe.

Jaworski, B. J., & Kohli, A. K. (1993). Market orientation: Antecedents and consequences, *Journal of Marketing Research, 57* (July), 53-70. Retrieved from http://www.jstor.org/discover/10.2307/1251854?uid=3739560&uid=2&uid=4&uid=3739256&sid=21101935055191

Jensen, A. R. (1982). The chronometry of intelligence. In R. J. Sternberg (Ed.), *Advances in the psychology of human intelligence* (Vol. 1, pp. 255-310). Hillsdale, NJ: Erlbaum.

Jensen, A. R. (1998). *The g factor*. Westport, CT: Praeger-Greenwood.

Johnson, B., & Christensen, L. (2012). *Educational research: Quantitative, qualitative, and mixed approaches*. (4th ed.). Thousand Oaks, CA: Sage Publications.

Johnson, M. D. (1998). *Customer orientation and market action*. Upper Saddle River, NJ: Prentice Hall.

Kara, A., Spillan, J. E., & DeShields, O. W. (2005). The effect of a market orientation on business performance: A study of small-sized service retailers using MARKOR scale. *Journal of Small Business Management, 43*(2), 105–118. doi: 10.1111/j.1540-627x.2005.00128.x

Kim, K., Kirkman, B. L., & Chen, G. (2008). Cultural intelligence and international assignment effectiveness: A conceptual model and preliminary findings. In S. Ang, & L. Van Dyne (Eds.), *Handbook of cultural intelligence: Theory, measurement, and applications* (pp. 71-90). Armonk, NY: M. E. Sharpe.

Kim, Y. J., & Van Dyne, L. (2012). Cultural intelligence and international leadership potential: The importance of contact for members of the majority. *Applied Psychology: An International Review, 61*: 272-294. Retrieved from http://culturalq.com/docs/APIR%202012%20Kim%20&%20Van%20Dyne.pdf

Kirca, A. H., & Hult, G. T. M. (2009). Intra-organizational factors and market orientation: effects of national culture. *International Marketing Review, 26*(6), 633-650. doi:10.1108/02651330911001323

Klafehn, J., Banerjee, P. M., & Chiu, C. (2008). Navigating cultures: The role of metacognitive cultural intelligence. In S. Ang, & L. Van Dyne (Eds.), *Handbook of cultural intelligence: Theory, measurement, and applications* (pp. 318-331). Armonk, NY: M. E. Sharpe.

Klopper, H. (2008). The qualitative research proposal. *Curationis, 31*(4), 62-72. Retrieved from http://www.curationis.org.za/index.php/curationis

Knab, E. F. (2008). *Going global: Success factors for penetrating emerging markets.* (Doctoral dissertation). Available from ProQuest Dissertations and Theses database. (UMI No. 3326207)

Kohli, A. K., & Jaworski, B. J. (1990). Market orientation: the construct, research propositions and managerial implications, *Journal of Marketing, 54* (2), 1-18. Retrieved from http://www.jstor.org/discover/10.2307/1251866?uid=3739560&uid=2&uid=4&uid=3739256&sid=21101935055191

Kohli, A. K., Jaworski, B. J., & Kumar, A. (1993). MARKOR: A measure of market orientation, *Journal of Marketing Research*, 30(4), 467–477. Retrieved from http://www.jstor.org/discover/10.2307/3172691?uid=3739560&uid=2&uid=4&uid=3739256&sid=21101935055191

Kumar, V., Jones, E., Venkatesan, R., & Leone, R. P. (2011). Is market orientation a source of sustainable competitive advantage or simply the cost of competing? *Journal of Marketing, 75*(1), 16-30. doi: 10.1509/jmkg.75.1.16

Lado, N., Maydeu-Olivares, A., & Rivera, J. (1998). Measuring Market orientation in several populations: A structural equations model. *European Journal of Marketing,* 32(1/2), 23 -39. doi: 10.1108/03090569810197408

Levitt, T. (1960). Marketing myopia. *Harvard Business Review, 38*(4), 45-56. Retrieved from http://hbr.org/magazine

Lin, C. H., & Kao, D. T. (2004, September). The impacts of Country-of-Origin on brand equity. *Journal of American Academy of Business, Cambridge,* 5(1/2), 37-40. Retrieved from http://www.jaabc.com/journal.htm

Lings, I. N., & Greenley, G. E. (2010). Internal market orientation and market-oriented behaviours. *Journal of Service Management, 21*(3), 321 – 343. doi: 10.1108/09564231011050788

Livermore, D. A. (2011). *The cultural intelligence difference: Master the one skill you can't do without in today's global economy.* New York, NY: AMACOM.

Livermore, D. A. (2010). *Leading with cultural intelligence: The new secret to success.* New York, NY: AMACOM.

Livermore, D. A. (2009). *Cultural intelligence: Improving your CQ to engage our multicultural world.* Grand Rapids, MI: Baker Academic.

Lovvorn, A. S., & Chen, J. S. (2011). Developing a global mindset: the relationship between an international assignment and cultural intelligence. *International Journal of Business and Social Science, 2* (9), 275-283. Retrieved from http://www.ijbssnet.com/journals/Vol._2_No._9_[Special_Issue_-_May_2011]/32.pdf

Lund Research Ltd. (2013). Purposive sampling explained. Retrieved from http://dissertation.laerd.com/purposive-sampling.php

MaCorr Research. (2013). Sample size calculator. Retrieved from http://www.macorr.com/sample-size-calculator.htm

Magnusson, P., Wilson, R. T., Zdravkovic, S., Zhou, J. X., & Westjohn, S. A. (2008). Breaking through the cultural clutter. *International Marketing Review, 25*(2), 183-201. doi:10.1108/02651330810866272

Mannor, M. J. (2008). Top executives and global leadership: At the intersection of cultural intelligence and strategic leadership theory. In S. Ang, & L. van Dyne (Eds.), *Handbook of cultural intelligence: Theory, measurement, and applications* (pp. 91-106). Armonk, NY: M. E. Sharpe.

Marber, P. (2009). *Seeing the elephant: Understanding globalization from trunk to tail.* Hoboken, NJ: John Wiley & Sons, Inc.

Matear, D. (2009). *An examination of cognitive, cultural, and emotional intelligences, and motivation in the development of global transformational leadership skills.* (Doctoral dissertation). Available from ProQuest Dissertations and Theses database. (UMI No. 3387673)

Matsumoto, D., & Hwang, H. C. (2013). Assessing cross-cultural competence: A review of available tests. *Journal of Cross-Cultural Psychology,* 44:849. doi: 10.1177/0022022113492891

Mavondo, F., & Farrell, M. (2003). Cultural orientation: Its relationship with market orientation, innovation and organisational performance. *Management Decision, 41*(3), 241 – 249. doi: 10.1108/00251740310468054

McGraw-Hill Companies. (2009, December 28). The 2009 Global Sourcebook. Engineering News Record. Retrieved from www.ENR.com.

McGraw-Hill Companies. (2010, December 20). The 2010 Global Sourcebook. Engineering News Record. Retrieved from www.ENR.com.

McGraw-Hill Companies. (2012, December 10). The 2010 Global Sourcebook. Engineering News Record. New York, NY: McGraw-Hill.

McNamara, C. P. (1972). The present status of the marketing concept. *Journal of Marketing, 36*(1), 50-57. Retrieved from http://www.jstor.org/discover/10.2307/1250868?uid=3739560&uid=2&uid=4&uid=3739256&sid=21101935055191

Minkov, M., & Hofstede, G. (2011). The evolution of Hofstede's doctrine. *Cross Cultural Management, 18*(1), 10-20. doi: 10.1108/13527601111104269

Monferrer, D., Blesa, A., & Ripollés, M. (2012). International market orientation and management capabilities as determinants of the new ventures' international behaviour. *Economics Research International, 2012*, 1-14. doi:10.1155/2012/623685

Multiple Intelligences Institute. (2008). MI Basics: The Theory. Retrieved at http://www.miinstitute.info/uploads/download/MI_Basics.pdf

Nakata, C., & Sivakumar, K. (2001). Instituting the marketing concept in a multinational setting: The role of national culture. *Journal of the Academy of Marketing Science, 29*(3), 255-275. doi: 10.1177/03079459994623

Narver, J. C., & Slater, S. F. (1990). The effect of market orientation on business profitability. *Journal of Marketing, 54*(4), 20-35. Retrieved from http://www.jstor.org/discover/10.2307/1251757?uid=3739560&uid=2&uid=4&uid=3739256&sid=21101935055191

Narver, J. C., & Slater, S. F. (1999). The effect of market orientation on business profitability. In R. Deshpandé (Ed.), *Developing a market orientation* (pp. 45-77). Thousand Oaks, CA: Sage Publications.

National Institute of Standards and Technology. (2000, August). Baldrige: A global approach for a global economy. *Baldrige National Quality Program, CEO Issue Sheet.* Retrieved from http://www.quality.nist.gov/Issue_Sheet_Global.htm

Neuman, W. L. (2006). *Social Research Methods: Qualitative and Quantitative Approaches.* (6th ed.). Boston, MA: Pearson Education.

Ng, K. Y., Tan, M. L., & Ang, S. (2011). Global culture capital and cosmopolitan human capital: The effects of global mindset and organizational routines on cultural intelligence and international experience. In A. Burton-Jones, & J. C. Spender. (Eds), *The Oxford handbook of human capital* (pp. 96-119). Oxford, U. K.: Oxford University Press.

Ng, K.,Van Dyne, L., & Ang, S. (2009). Beyond international experience: The strategic role of cultural intelligence for executive selection in international human resource management. In P.R. Sparrow (Ed.), *Handbook of International HR Research: Integrating People, Process, and Context* (pp. 97-113). Oxford: Blackwell.

Ng, S. I., Lee, J. A., & Soutar, G. N. (2007). Are Hofstedes and Schwartz's value frameworks congruent? *International Marketing Review, 24*(2), 164-180. doi:10.1108/02651330710741802

Nisbett, R. E. (2003). *The geography of thought: Why we think the way we do.* New York, NY: Free Press.

Nummela, N., Saarenketo, S., & Puumalainen, K. (2004). A global mindset - A prerequisite for successful internationalization? *Canadian Journal of Administrative Sciences, 21*(1), 51-64. doi: 10.1111/j.1936-4490.2004.tb00322.x

Olavarrieta, S., & Friedmann, R. (2008). Market orientation, knowledge-related resources and firm performance. *Journal of Business Research, 61*(6), 623-630. doi: 10.1016/j.jbusres.2007.06.037

Onwuegbuzie, A. J. (2000, November 21). *Expanding the framework of internal and external validity in quantitative research.* Paper presented at the Annual Meeting of the Association for the Advancement of Educational Research (AAER), Ponte Vedra, FL.

Oolders, T., Chernyshenko, O. S., & Stark, S. (2008). Cultural intelligence as a mediator of relationships between openness to experience and adaptive performance. In S. Ang, & L. Van Dyne (Eds.), *Handbook of cultural intelligence: Theory, measurement, and applications* (pp. 145-158). Armonk, NY: M. E. Sharpe.

Osayomi, T. S. (2007). *International marketing research.* School of Business and Economics, Atlantic International University (Florida). Retrieved from http://itica.aiu.edu/applications/DocumentLibraryManager/upload/Public%20Government%20Relations.pdf

Parsons, T. (1951). *The social system.* New York, NY: Free Press.

Pearl, M. (2007). Creating a competitive edge: The value of cross-industry knowledge. *Business Strategy Series, 8*(2), 142-147. doi:10.1108/17515630710685203

Pearl, M. (2009). Going global: How to make the decision. *Manufacturing Today, 9*(1), 10-13. Retrieved from http://www.manufacturing-today.com/

Plum, E. (2008). *Cultural intelligence: The art of leading cultural complexity.* London, England: Middlesex University Press.

Plunkett, J. W. (2010, April 23). Introduction to the Engineering & Research Industry. [Electronic version]. *Engineering & Research Industry.* Retrieved from http://www.plunkettresearchonline.com.

Plunkett Research Ltd. (2013, March 22). Guide to the Engineering Industry. [Electronic version]. *Engineering & Research Industry.* Retrieved from http://www.plunkettresearch.com.

Prahalad, C. K. (1997). The work of new age managers in the emerging competitive landscape. In F. Hesselbein, M. Goldsmith, & R. Beckhard. (Eds). *The organization of the future* (pp. 159-168). San Francisco: Jossey-

Bass.

Randolph, K. A., & Myers, L. L. (2013). *Basic statistics in multivariate analysis.* Oxford University Press: New York, NY.

Robinson, D., & Harvey, M. (2008). Global leadership in a culturally diverse world. *Management Decision, 46*(3), 466-480. doi:10.1108/00251740810863898

Rockstuhl, T., Hong, Y.Y., Ng, K.Y., Ang, S., & Chiu, C.Y. (2010). The culturally intelligent brain: From detecting to bridging cultural differences. *NeuroLeadership Institute, 3*: 1-15. Retrieved from http://culturalq.com/docs/Rockstuhl_et_al_2010.pdf

Rockstuhl, T., Seiler, S., Ang, S., Van Dyne, L., & Annen, H. (2011). Beyond general intelligence (IQ) and emotional intelligence (EQ): the role of cultural intelligence (CQ) on cross-border leadership effectiveness in a globalized world. *Journal of Social Issues, 67*(4), 825—840. doi: 10.1111/j.1540-4560.2011.01730.x

Rogers, P. S. (2008). The challenge of behavioral cultural intelligence: what might dialogue tell us? In S. Ang, & L. Van Dyne (Eds.), *Handbook of cultural intelligence: Theory, measurement, and applications* (pp. 243-256). Armonk, NY: M. E. Sharpe.

Ruekert, R. W. (1992). Developing a market orientation: An organizational strategy perspective. *International Journal of Research in Marketing, 9,* 225-245. doi: 10.1016/0167-8116(92)90019-H

Salkind, N. J. (2003). *Exploring research.* (5th ed.). Upper Saddle River, NJ: Prentice Hall.

Sanzo, M. J., Santos, M. L., Vázquez, R., & Álvarez, L. I. (2003) The role of market orientation in business dyadic relationships: Testing an integrator model. *Journal of Marketing Management, 19*(1/2), 73-107. doi:10.1080/0267257X.2003.9728202

Sarason, S. B., & Doris, J. (1979). *Educational handicap, public policy, and social history.* New York, NY: Free Press.

Schaffer, M., & Miller, G. (2008). Cultural intelligence: A key success factor for expatriates. In S. Ang, & L. Van Dyne (Eds.), *Handbook of cultural intelligence: Theory, measurement, and applications* (pp. 107-125). Armonk, NY: M. E. Sharpe.

Schlosser, F. (2004). *The market-oriented contribution of individuals: Translating strategy into action* (Doctoral dissertation). Available from ProQuest Dissertations and Theses database. (UMI No. NR01263)

Schlosser, F., & McNaughton, R. (2009). Using the I-MARKOR scale to identify market-oriented individuals in the financial services sector. *The Journal of Services Marketing, 23*(4), 236-248. doi: 10.1108/08876040910965575

Scholl, D. (2009). *The relationship between cultural intelligence and the performance of multinational teams.* (Doctoral dissertation). Available from ProQuest

Dissertations and Theses database. (UMI No. 3381839)

Scholte, J. A. (2005). *Globalization: A critical introduction* (2nd ed.). New York, NY: Palgrave Macmillan.

Schwartz, S. H. (1994). Beyond individualism/collectivism: new cultural dimensions of values. In U. Kim, H. C. Triandis, C. Kagitcibasi, S. C. Choi, & G. Yoon. (Eds), *Individualism and collectivism: Theory, method and applications* (pp. 85-119). Thousand Oaks: CA, Sage Publications.

Schwartz, S. H. (1999). A Theory of Cultural Values and Some Implications for Work. *Applied Psychology: An International Review, 48*(1), 23-47. doi:10.1080/026999499377655

Schwartz, S. H., & Bardi, A. (2001, May). Value hierarchies across cultures: Taking a similarities perspective. *Journal of Cross-Cultural Psychology, 32*, 268-290. doi: 10.1177/0022022101032003002

Shapiro, B. P. (1988). What the hell is 'market oriented?'. *Harvard Business Review*, 66 (6), 119-125. Retrieved from http://nts2.ximb.ac.in/users/fac/MNT/mnt.nsf/dd5cab6801f1723585 256474005327c8/9ef3ec6c75b864eb652576f0001c62dc/$FILE/What %20the%20hell%20is%20Market%20Oriented.pdf

Shi, X., & Wang, J. (2011). Interpreting Hofstede model and GLOBE model: Which way to go for cross-cultural research? *International Journal of Business and Management, 6*(5), 93-99. Retrieved from http://journal.ccsenet.org/index.php/ijbm/article/viewFile/10431/74 48

Shokef, E., & Erez, M. (2008). Cultural intelligence and global identity in multicultural teams. In S. Ang, & L. Van Dyne (Eds.), *Handbook of cultural intelligence: Theory, measurement, and applications* (pp. 177-191). Armonk, NY: M. E. Sharpe.

Sivakumar, K., & Nakata, C. (2001). The stampede toward Hofstede's framework: Avoiding the sample design pit in cross-cultural research. *Journal of International Business Studies, 32*(3), 555-574. Retrieved from http://www.jstor.org/discover/10.2307/3069497?uid=3739560&uid= 2134&uid=2&uid=70&uid=4&uid=3739256&sid=21101935055191

Smith, P. B., Dugan, S., & Trompenaars, F. (1996). National culture and the values of organizational employees: A dimensional analysis across 43 nations. *Journal of Cross-Cultural Psychology, 27*(2), 231-264. doi: 10.1177/0022022196272006

Spearman, C. (1927). *The abilities of man: Their nature and measurement*. St. Martin's Street, London: Macmillan and Company.

Sternberg, R. J. (1985). *Beyond IQ: A triarchic theory of human intelligence*. New York: Cambridge University Press.

Sternberg, R. J. (2000). Patterns of giftedness: A triarchic analysis. *Roeper Review, 22*(4), 231-231. doi: 10.1080/02783190009554044

Sternberg, R. J. (2007). Intelligence and culture. In S. Kitayama & D. Cohen

(Eds.), *Handbook of cultural psychology* (pp. 547-568). New York, NY: Guilford Press.

Sternberg, R. J., & Detterman, D. K. (1986). *What is intelligence? Contemporary viewpoints on its nature and definition.* Norwood, NJ: Ablex.

Sternberg, R. J., Forsythe, G. B., Hedlund, J., Horvath, J. A., Wagner, R. K., Williams, W. M., Snook, S. A., & Grigorenko, E. L. (2000). *Practical intelligence in everyday life.* New York: Cambridge University Press.

Sternberg, R. J., & Grigorenko, E. L. (2006). Cultural intelligence and successful intelligence. *Group and Organization Management, 31* (1), 27-39. doi: 10.1177/1059601105275255

Stoelhorst, J. W., & van Raaij, E. M. (2004). On explaining performance differentials: Marketing and the managerial theory of the firm, *Journal of Business Research, 57*(5), 462-477. doi: 10.1016/S0148-2963(02)00313-2

Stonehouse, G., Campbell, D., Hamill, J., & Purdie, T. (2004). *Global and transnational business: Strategy and management.* (2nd ed.). West Sussex, UK: John Wiley & Sons.

Stuart, R. B. (2004). Twelve practical suggestions for achieving multicultural competence. *Professional Psychology: Research and Practice, 35*(1), 3-9. doi: 10.1037/0735-7028.35.1.3

Symonds, J. E., & Gorard, S. (2010). Death of mixed methods? Or the rebirth of research as a craft. *Evaluation & Research in Education, 23*(2), 121-136. doi: 10.1080/09500790.2010.483514

Templar, K. J., Tay, C., & Chandrasekar, N. A. (2006). Motivational cultural intelligence, realistic job previews, realistic living conditions preview, and cross-cultural adjustment. *Group and Organization Management, 31*(1), 154-173. doi: 10.1177/1059601105275293

Thomas, D. C. (2006). Domain and development of cultural intelligence: the importance of mindfulness. *Group and Organization Management, 31*(1), 78-99. doi: 10.1177/1059601105275266

Thomas, D. C., & Inkson, K. (2003). *People skills for global business: Cultural intelligence.* San Francisco, CA: Berrett-Koehler Publishers.

Thomas, D. C., & Inkson, K. (2009). *Cultural intelligence: Living and working globally.* (2nd ed.). San Francisco, CA: Berrett-Koehler Publishers.

Tichy, N. M., & DeRose, C. (2006). Leadership judgment at the front line. In F. Hesselbein & M. Goldsmith (Eds.), *The leader of the future 2: Visions, strategies, and practices for the new era* (pp. 191-205). San Francisco, CA: Jossey-Bass.

Tomášková, E. (2009). The current methods of measurement of market orientation. *European Research Studies, 12*(3), 135-150. Retrieved from http://www.ersj.eu/

Tongco, M. D. C. (2007). Purposive sampling as a tool for informant selection. *Ethnobotany Research & Applications, 5* (147-158). Retrieved from http://scholarspace.manoa.hawaii.edu/bitstream/handle/10125/227/I 1547-3465-05-147.pdf?sequence=4

Triola, M. F. (2005). *Essentials of statistics.* (2nd ed.). Boston, MA: Pearson Education.

Trompenaars, F., & Hampden-Turner, C. (1998). *Riding the waves of culture: Understanding diversity in global business* (2nd ed.). New York, NY: McGraw-Hill.

Trustrum, L. B. (1989). Marketing: Concept and function. *European Journal of Marketing, 23*(3), 48-56. doi: 10.1108/EUM0000000000560

Tschida, M. H. (2010). *The impact of market orientation on the performance of professional service firms.* (Doctoral thesis, Norwich Business School, University of East Anglia). Retrieved from https://ueaeprints.uea.ac.uk/10589/1/Thesis_tschida_m_2010.pdf.

Tucker, R. W. (2000). International marketing. In Mahoney, W. D. (Ed.), *Marketing handbook for the design and construction professional: Society for marketing professional services,* (pp. 65-74). Los Angeles, CA: BNi Publications.

Tung, R. L., & Miller, E. L. (1990). Managing in the twenty-first century: The need for global orientation. *Management International Review, 30*(1), 5-18. Retrieved from http://www.jstor.org/discover/10.2307/40228002?uid=3739560&uid=2134&uid=2&uid=70&uid=4&uid=3739256&sid=21101935055191

Valenti, M. (1995). Engineering across the seas. *Mechanical Engineering, 117*(6), 52-58. Retrieved from http://memagazine.asme.org/

Van Dyne, L., Ang S., & Koh, C. K. S. (2009). Cultural intelligence: Measurement and scale development. In M. A. Moodian (Ed.), *Contemporary leadership and intercultural competence: Exploring the cross-cultural dynamics within organizations* (pp. 233-254). Thousand Oaks, CA: Sage Publications.

Van Dyne, L., Ang, S., & Koh, C. (2008). Development and validation of the CQS: The cultural intelligence scale. In S. Ang, & L. Van Dyne (Eds.), *Handbook of cultural intelligence: Theory, measurement, and applications* (pp. 16-38). Armonk, NY: M. E. Sharpe.

Van Dyne, L., Ang, S., & Livermore, D. (2010). Cultural intelligence: A pathway for leading in a rapidly globalizing world. In K. Hannum, B. B. McFeeters, & L. Booysen (Eds.), *Leading across differences* (pp. 131-138). San Francisco, CA: Pfeiffer.

Vázquez, R., Santos, M. L., & Álvarez, L. I. (2001). Market orientation, innovation and competitive strategies in industrial firms. *Journal of Strategic Marketing, 9*(1), 69-90. doi: 10.1080/09652540123013

Venaik, S., & Brewer, P. (2010). Avoiding uncertainty in Hofstede and GLOBE. *Journal of International Business Studies, 41*(8), 1294-1315. doi:10.1057/jibs.2009.96

Vernon, P. E. (1971). *The structure of human abilities*. London, UK: Methuen.

Vieth, C. S., & Smith, T. W. (2008, February). Engineering and technical leadership development: Challenges in a rapidly changing global market. *Chief Learning Officer*, 7(2), 46-49. Retrieved from http://clomedia.com/

Vytlacil, L. L. (2010). *Market orientation and business performance: The role of positional advantage*(Doctoral dissertation). Available from ProQuest Dissertations and Theses database. (UMI No. 3439658)

Waclawski, J. (2002). Large-scale organizational change and performance: An empirical examination. *Human Resource Development Quarterly*, 13(3), 289-305. doi: 10.1002/hrdq.1032

Ward, C., & Fischer, R. (2008). Personality, cultural intelligence, and cross-cultural adaptation. In S. Ang, & L. Van Dyne (Eds.), *Handbook of cultural intelligence: Theory, measurement, and applications* (pp. 159-173). Armonk, NY: M. E. Sharpe.

Webster Jr., F. E. (1988). The Rediscovery of the marketing concept. *Business Horizons*, 31(3), 29-39. doi: 10.1016/0007-6813(88)90006-7

Weick, K., & Sutcliffe, K. (2007). *Managing the unexpected*. (2nd ed.). San Francisco, CA: Jossey-Bass.

Wilson, S. D. (2004). *The relationship between leadership and domains of multiple intelligences* (Doctoral dissertation). Available from ProQuest Dissertations and Theses database. (UMI No. 3151206)

Wren, D. A. (2005). *The history of management thought* (5th ed.). Hoboken, NJ: John Wiley & Sons, Inc.

Yaprak, A. (2008). Culture study in international marketing: a critical review and suggestions for future research. *International Marketing Review*, 25(2), 215-229. doi:10.1108/02651330810866290

Yip, G. S. (2003). Global strategy…in a world of nations. In H. Mintzberg, J. Lampel, J. B. Quinn, & S. Ghoshal (Eds). *The strategy process: Concepts, contexts, cases.* (pp. 280-288). Upper Saddle River, NJ: Prentice Hall.

Zhu, T. (2011). Focusing on managers and employees in strategy research: Intra firm network centrality & individual employee's market orientation. *AMA Summer Educators' Conference Proceedings*, 22, 67. Retrieved from http://www.marketingpower.com/community/arc/pages/connections/conferences/proceedings.aspx

APPENDIX A
INFORMED CONSENT FORM

Appendix A

Informed Consent Form

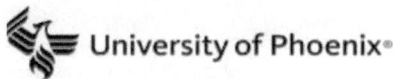

INFORMED CONSENT: PARTICIPANTS 18 YEARS OF AGE AND OLDER

Dear Participant,

My name is Stephen R. Galati and I am a student at the University of Phoenix working on a doctoral degree. I am doing a research study entitled *Entering the Global Engineering Market: A Correlational Study of Cultural Intelligence and Market Orientation*. The purpose of the research study is to determine any relationship that may exist between the factors of cultural intelligence and individual market orientation in the context of U.S.-based engineering firms entering the global marketplace.

Your participation will involve completing two surveys and answering some demographic questions. The questionnaires will take approximately 20 minutes to complete. You can decide to be a part of this study or not. Once you start, you can withdraw from the study at any time without any penalty, loss of privacy, or loss of benefits. The results of the research study may be published. Your identity will remain confidential and your name will not be made known to any outside party.

In this research, there are no foreseeable risks to you.

Although there may be no direct benefit to you, a possible benefit from your being part of this study is that the research may lead to more awareness about cultural intelligence and global market orientation.

If you have any questions about the research study, please call me at (207) 485-1901 or email me at sgalati1026@email.phoenix.edu. If you wish to withdraw from the study, you may do so at any time by emailing me with your withdrawal request. Any withdrawal request must include your personal identification number (PIN), which you will assign at the start of the survey. For questions about your rights as a study participant, or any concerns or complaints, please contact the University of Phoenix Institutional Review Board via email at IRB@phoenix.edu.

As a participant in this study, you should understand the following:
1. You may decide not to be part of this study or you may want to withdraw from the study at any time. If you want to withdraw, you can do so without any problems.
2. Your identity will be kept confidential.

3. Stephen R. Galati, the researcher, has fully explained the nature of the research study and has answered all of your questions and concerns.
4. Data will be kept in a secure and locked area. The data will be kept for five years, and then destroyed.
5. The results of this study may be published.

"By signing this form, you agree that you understand the nature of the study, the possible risks to you as a participant, and how your identity will be kept confidential. When you sign this form, this means that you are 18 years old or older and that you give your permission to volunteer as a participant in the study that is described here."

Return of the signed form can be completed in one of three ways:
1) Faxing the signed form to (207) 293-4693;
2) Emailing a scan of the signed form to *sgalati1026@email.phoenix.edu*; or
3) Mailing the signed form to: Galati-Consent Form, 14 Gabriel Drive, Augusta, Maine 04330.

(☐) I accept the above terms.   (☐) I do not accept the above terms. (CHECK ONE)

_____   _____   _____
Participant Signature   **Participant Name (Print)**   **Date**

_____   **Stephen R. Galati**   _____
Researcher Signature   **Researcher Name**   **Date**

APPENDIX B
SURVEYMONKEY PERMISSION

Non-Disclosure Agreement

SurveyMonkey.com, LLC ("**SurveyMonkey**") acknowledges that in order to provide the services to Stephen R. Galati (hereinafter "**Researcher**") who is a researcher in a confidential study with the University of Phoenix, Inc., SurveyMonkey must agree to keep the information obtained as part of its services (as more fully described below) confidential. Therefore the parties agree as follows:

1. The information to be disclosed under this Non-disclosure Agreement ("**Agreement**") is described as follows and shall be considered "Confidential Information": (a) all information obtained during the course of the study which is provided to SurveyMonkey; (b) all of Researcher's survey data; and (c) the responses of **100** completed surveys. Notwithstanding the foregoing, Confidential Information is limited to Researcher's information contained in the SurveyMonkey Account associated with the username: **sgalati1026** (the "**Account**"). All Confidential Information remains the property of Researcher.

2. SurveyMonkey agrees to disclose Confidential Information to its employees, contractors, affiliates, advisors or agents, (collectively, "**Representatives**") on a need to know basis and to use the Confidential Information for STATISTICAL ANALYSIS only and for no other purposes.

3. SurveyMonkey further agrees to keep in confidence and not disclose any Confidential Information to a third party or parties for a period of three (3) years from the date of such disclosure. All oral disclosures of Confidential Information as well as written disclosures of the Confidential Information are covered by this Agreement.

4. Despite anything to the contrary in this Agreement, any Confidential Information associated with or contained in the Account (including survey data) is subject to the SurveyMonkey Privacy Policy located at http://www.surveymonkey.com/mp/policy/privacy-policy (as may be amended from time to time) (the "**Privacy Policy**"). This Agreement shall not prohibit SurveyMonkey from using the Confidential Information in any manner permitted by the Privacy Policy. The Privacy Policy will prevail over this Agreement in the event of any conflict between the two, but only to the extent required to resolve such conflict.

5. SurveyMonkey shall, upon Researcher's request either destroy or return the Confidential Information upon termination of this Agreement with the exception of copies made as part of computer backups made solely for disaster recovery purposes.

6. Any obligation of SurveyMonkey under this Agreement shall not apply to Confidential Information that:

    a) Is or becomes a part of the public knowledge through no fault of SurveyMonkey;
    b) SurveyMonkey can demonstrate was independently developed without reference to Researcher's Confidential Information;
    c) SurveyMonkey can demonstrate was rightfully in its possession before disclosure by Researcher or research subjects; or

Current version 032012

d) SurveyMonkey can demonstrate was rightfully received from a third party who was not Researcher or a research subject and was not under confidentiality restriction on disclosure and without breach of any nondisclosure obligation.

7. SurveyMonkey agrees to obligate its Representatives, if any, who have access to any portion of Confidential Information to protect the confidential nature of the Confidential Information with reasonable care.

8. In the event SurveyMonkey receives a subpoena or other legal information request and believes it has a legal obligation to disclose Confidential Information, SurveyMonkey will notify Researcher promptly of such legal information request to the extent permitted by law. If Researcher objects to the release of such Confidential Information, SurveyMonkey will allow Researcher, at his own expense, to exercise any legal rights or remedies regarding the release and protection of the Confidential Information.

9. SurveyMonkey expressly acknowledges and agrees that the breach, or threatened breach, by it through a disclosure of Confidential Information may cause irreparable harm and that Researcher may not have an adequate remedy at law. Therefore, SurveyMonkey agrees that upon such breach, or threatened breach, Researcher will be entitled to seek injunctive relief to prevent SurveyMonkey from commencing or continuing any action constituting such breach without showing or providing evidence of actual damage.

10. This Agreement shall be governed by the laws of the State of California, without regard to its conflict of laws principles. The parties submit to the exclusive jurisdiction of the state courts located in Santa Clara County, California and the federal courts located in the Northern District of California.

11. The parties to this Agreement agree that a copy of the original signature (including an electronic copy) may be used for any and all purposes for which the original signature may have been used. The parties further waive any right to challenge the admissibility or authenticity of this document in a court of law based solely on the absence of an original signature.

IN WITNESS WHEREOF, each of the undersigned has caused this Agreement to be duly executed in its name and on its behalf:

Printed Name of Third Party/Vendor: SurveyMonkey.com, LLC
Signature:
Address: 285 Hamilton Avenue, Suite 500, Palo Alto, California, 94301
Date: 03-04-2013

Printed Name of Researcher: Stephen R. Galati
Signature:
Address: 437 Belgrade Road, Mount Vernon, Maine 04352
Date: February 28, 2013

Current version 032012

PREMISES, RECRUITMENT AND NAME (PRN) USE PERMISSION
SurveyMonkey (SurveyMonkey.com, LLC)

Name of Facility, Organization, University, Institution, or Association

Please complete the following by check marking any permissions listed here that you approve, and please provide your signature, title, date, and organizational information below. If you have any questions or concerns about this research study, please contact the University of Phoenix Institutional Review Board via email at IRB@phoenix.edu.

☐ I hereby authorize [Insert name], a student of University of Phoenix, to use the premises (facility identified below) to conduct a study entitled [Insert name of study].

X I hereby authorize Stephen R. Galati, a student of University of Phoenix, to recruit subjects for participation in a study entitled **Entering the Global Engineering Market: A Correlational Study of Cultural Intelligence and Market Orientation**.

X I hereby authorize Stephen R. Galati, a student of University of Phoenix, to use the name of the facility, organization, university, institution, or association identified above when publishing results from the study entitled **Entering the Global Engineering Market: A Correlational Study of Cultural Intelligence and Market Orientation**.

Signature *Stephen R Galati* / *[signature]*
Name Noreen Bergin

Date 02/28/2013 / 03/04/2013

Title VP, Finance

Address of Organization:

285 Hamilton Avenue, Suite 500, Palo Alto, CA, 94301

APPENDIX C
PERMISSION TO USE EXISTING SURVEYS

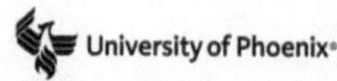

PERMISSION TO USE AN EXISTING SURVEY

Date **March 18, 2013**

From: Author Name: Linn Van Dyne, Ph.D.
Author Address: The Eli Broad Graduate School of Management
Michigan State University
N475 Business College Complex
East Lansing MI 48824-1122

To: Researcher Name: Mr. Stephen R. Galati

Thank you for your request for permission to use the Cultural Intelligence Scale (CQS) survey instrument in your research study. We are willing to allow you to access, use and reproduce the above named instrument at no charge with the following understanding and in accordance with the following terms and conditions:

- You will use this survey only for your research study and will not sell or use it with any compensated management or curriculum development activities.
- You will include the copyright statement on all copies of the instrument.
- You will send your research study and one copy of reports, articles, and related publications that make use of this survey data promptly to our attention.

If these are acceptable terms and conditions, please indicate so by signing one copy of this letter and returning it to us.

Sincerely,

Linn Van Dyne, Ph.D.
Author Name (please print)

_____   3-20-2013
Author Signature   Date

I understand these conditions and agree to abide by these terms and conditions.

_____   March 18, 2013
Stephen R. Galati - Researcher   Date
University of Phoenix

Expected date of completion **04/2014**

Current version 032012

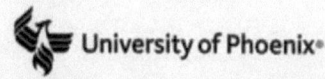

PERMISSION TO USE AN EXISTING SURVEY

Date **March 18, 2013**

From: Author Name: Francine Schlosser, Ph.D.
Author Address: Associate Professor, Odette School of Business,
Director, Centre for Enterprise and Law
University of Windsor
360 Sunset Avenue
Windsor, ON N9B 3P4

To: Researcher Name: Mr. Stephen R. Galati

Thank you for your request for permission to use the I-MARKOR survey instrument in your research study. We are willing to allow you to access, use and reproduce the above named instrument at no charge with the following understanding and in accordance with the following terms and conditions:

- You will use this survey only for your research study and will not sell or use it with any compensated management or curriculum development activities.
- You will include the copyright statement on all copies of the instrument.
- You will send your research study and one copy of reports, articles, and related publications that make use of this survey data promptly to our attention.

If these are acceptable terms and conditions, please indicate so by signing one copy of this letter and returning it to us.

Sincerely,

Francine Schlosser, Ph.D.
Author Name (please print)

_____   Ma 20/13
Author Signature   Date

I understand these conditions and agree to abide by these terms and conditions.

_____   March 18, 2013
Stephen R. Galati - Researcher   Date
University of Phoenix

Expected date of completion **04/2014**

Current version 032012

APPENDIX D
SURVEY INSTRUMENTS

The 20-item four factor CQS (the CQ Scale)

		Strongly DISAGREE						Strongly AGREE

CQ-Strategy:

MC1	I am conscious of the cultural knowledge I use when interacting with people with different cultural backgrounds.	1 2 3 4 5 6 7
MC2	I adjust my cultural knowledge as I interact with people from a culture that is unfamiliar to me.	1 2 3 4 5 6 7
MC3	I am conscious of the cultural knowledge I apply to cross-cultural interactions.	1 2 3 4 5 6 7
MC4	I check the accuracy of my cultural knowledge as I interact with people from different cultures.	1 2 3 4 5 6 7

CQ-Knowledge:

COG1	I know the legal and economic systems of other cultures.	1 2 3 4 5 6 7
COG2	I know the rules (e.g., vocabulary, grammar) of other languages.	1 2 3 4 5 6 7
COG3	I know the cultural values and religious beliefs of other cultures.	1 2 3 4 5 6 7
COG4	I know the marriage systems of other cultures.	1 2 3 4 5 6 7
COG5	I know the arts and crafts of other cultures.	1 2 3 4 5 6 7
COG6	I know the rules for expressing non-verbal behaviors in other cultures.	1 2 3 4 5 6 7

CQ-Motivation:

MOT1	I enjoy interacting with people from different cultures.	1 2 3 4 5 6 7
MOT2	I am confident that I can socialize with locals in a culture that is unfamiliar to me	1 2 3 4 5 6 7
MOT3	I am sure I can deal with the stresses of adjusting to a culture that is new to me.	1 2 3 4 5 6 7
MOT4	I enjoy living in cultures that are unfamiliar to me.	1 2 3 4 5 6 7
MOT5	I am confident that I can get used to the shopping conditions in a different culture.	1 2 3 4 5 6 7

CQ-Behavior:

BEH1	I change my verbal behavior (e.g., accent, tone) when a cross-cultural interaction requires it.	1 2 3 4 5 6 7
BEH2	I use pause and silence differently to suit different cross-cultural situations.	1 2 3 4 5 6 7
BEH3	I vary the rate of my speaking when a cross-cultural situation requires it.	1 2 3 4 5 6 7
BEH4	I change my non-verbal behavior when a cross-cultural situation requires it.	1 2 3 4 5 6 7
BEH5	I alter my facial expressions when a cross-cultural interaction requires it.	1 2 3 4 5 6 7

Copyright © Cultural Intelligence Center 2005. Used by permission of the Cultural Intelligence Center. All rights reserved.

Note: Use of this scale is granted to academic researchers for research purposes only. For information on using the scale for purposes other than academic research (e.g., consultants and non-academic organizations), please send an email to cquery@culturalq.com.

For additional information see Ang, S., Van Dyne, L., Koh, C.K.S., Ng, K.Y., Templer, K.J., Tay, C., & Chandrasekar, N.A. (2007). Cultural intelligence: Its measurement and effects on cultural judgment and decision making, cultural adaptation, and task performance. Management and Organization Review, 3, 335-371.

I-MARKOR

The following questions refer to customers and distributors. In this survey, a "customer" refers to the individual that pays the premium, whereas a "distributor" refers to an independent or captive sales agency, managing general agent, producing general agent, or other business partners that deal directly with the customer.

For each item in the following section please answer first whether you feel obligated to do this (I should) and then whether you actually do this (I do). For example, when your manager or company has informally communicated this expectation, or your own experiences have highlighted its importance, you would reflect this by ranking the item highly on "I should". However, if you don't actually do this action (perhaps because you don't have enough resources, time, or just have personal reasons for not wanting to do it) then you would answer "I do" relatively lower on the scale.

1. Never	2. Almost never	3. Sometimes	4. Often	5. Almost Always

1. Interact with agencies to find out what products or services customers will need in the future.
   I should 1 2 3 4 5
   I do 1 2 3 4 5

2. Ask distributors to assess the quality of our products and services.
   I should 1 2 3 4 5
   I do 1 2 3 4 5

3. Talk to or survey those who can influence our customers' purchases (e.g., distributors).
   I should 1 2 3 4 5
   I do 1 2 3 4 5

4. Collect industry information through informal means (e.g., lunch with industry friends, talks with trade partners).
   I should 1 2 3 4 5
   I do 1 2 3 4 5

5. Take responsibility to detect fundamental shifts in our industry (e.g., competition, technology, regulation) in my communication with distributors.
   I should 1 2 3 4 5
   I do 1 2 3 4 5

6. In my communication with distributors, periodically review the likely effect of changes in our business environment (e.g., company mergers and acquisitions) on customers.
   I should 1 2 3 4 5
   I do 1 2 3 4 5

7. Participate in informal "hall talk" that concerns our competitor's tactics or strategies.
   I should 1 2 3 4 5
   I do 1 2 3 4 5

8. Participate in interdepartmental meetings to discuss market trends and developments.
   I should 1 2 3 4 5
   I do 1 2 3 4 5

9. Try to circulate documents (e.g., emails, reports, newsletters) that provide information on my distributor contacts and their customers to appropriate departments.
   I should 1 2 3 4 5
   I do 1 2 3 4 5

10. Let appropriate departments know when I find out that something important has happened to a major distributor or market.
    I should 1 2 3 4 5
    I do 1 2 3 4 5

11. Communicate with our marketing department concerning market developments.
    I should 1 2 3 4 5
    I do 1 2 3 4 5

12. Review our product development efforts with distributors to ensure that they are in line with what customers want.
    I should 1 2 3 4 5
    I do 1 2 3 4 5

13. Pass on information that could help company decision-makers to review changes taking place in our business environment.
    I should 1 2 3 4 5
    I do 1 2 3 4 5

14. Coordinate my activities with the activities of coworkers or departments in this organisation.
    I should 1 2 3 4 5
    I do 1 2 3 4 5

15	Take action when I find out that customers are unhappy with the quality of our service.	I should 1 2 3 4 5
		I do 1 2 3 4 5
16	Communicate market developments to departments other than marketing.	I should 1 2 3 4 5
		I do 1 2 3 4 5
17	Try to help distributors achieve their goals.	I should 1 2 3 4 5
		I do 1 2 3 4 5
18	Try to bring a customer with a problem together with a product or person that helps the customer to solve that problem.	I should 1 2 3 4 5
		I do 1 2 3 4 5
19	Respond quickly if a distributor has any problems with our offerings	I should 1 2 3 4 5
		I do 1 2 3 4 5
20	Jointly develop solutions for customers with members of our customer / advisor relationship team	I should 1 2 3 4 5
		I do 1 2 3 4 5

APPENDIX E
DEMOGRAPHIC SURVEY

Appendix E

Demographic Survey

Thank you for agreeing to participate in this survey. Please answer the following demographic questions using responses that best describe you:

1. Please enter your assigned six alphanumeric character research Personal Identification Number (PIN) if you wish to have the option of withdrawing and deleting your responses from the study at any time. Alphanumeric characters include lowercase alphabetic letters (a-z), uppercase alphabetic letters (A-Z), and single digit whole numbers (0-9). The PIN was included in the email inviting you to participate in the study.

   RESEARCH PIN: ☐ ☐ ☐ ☐ ☐ ☐

2. What is your gender?

   Male   Female

3. What is your age?

   Under 21   21-30   31-40   41-50
   51-60   61-70   71-80   Over 80

4. What is your ethnic background?

   Hispanic / Latino   Non-Hispanic / Latino

5. What is your race?

   White / Caucasian / European   Black / African

   South Asian (Indian Subcontinent)   East Asian (China, Korea, Japan, Thailand, etc.)

   Native American   Middle Eastern

Pacific Islander   Other

6. How long have you been in your current role?

    Less than 1 year   1-2 years   3-5 years

    6-10 years   11-15 years   16-20 years

    More than 20 years

7. How long have you been in your current company (including all previously acquired or merged companies)?

    Less than 1 year   1-2 years   3-5 years

    6-10 years   11-15 years   16-20 years

    More than 20 years

8. What type of engineering do you market globally? (Choose all that apply)

    Acoustical   Aerospace   Agricultural

    Biomedical   Biomolecular   Chemical

    Civil   Computer/Software   Electrical

    Environmental   Geotechnical   Green / Sustainability

    Industrial   Manufacturing   Materials

    Mechanical   Minerals / Mining   Nanoengineering

    Nuclear   Oceanic   Petroleum

    Power   Process   Seismic

    Structural   Traffic   Transportation

APPENDIX F
PARTICIPANT
ENGAGEMENT EMAIL

Appendix F

Participant Engagement Email

Dear _____:

My name is Stephen R. Galati and I am a student at the University of Phoenix working on a doctoral degree. I am inviting you to participate in my research study entitled *Entering the Global Engineering Market: A Correlational Study of Cultural Intelligence and Market Orientation*. You were selected as a possible participant because of your current leadership position in a successful global or international design firm.

Purpose of the Study

The purpose of the research study is to determine any relationship that may exist between the independent variables of cultural intelligence and individual market orientation of decision makers at U.S.-based engineering firms to the dependent variable of entering the global marketplace.

What will Participation Entail?

Your participation will involve completing two surveys and answering some demographic questions. The questionnaires will take approximately 20 minutes to complete. Once you start, you can withdraw from the study at any time without any penalty, loss of privacy, or loss of benefits. The results of the research study may be published but your identity will remain confidential and your name will not be made known to any outside party.

Participation in the study is voluntary and strictly confidential. There is no charge for participation. As compensation, participants will receive a complimentary copy of the study findings once completed and accepted by the University.

Procedure to Participate

If you agree to participate in the study, please click on the below link to read and either accept or decline the Informed Consent Form. Acceptance requires a signed Informed Consent Form be returned. Please read this form carefully and feel free to ask any questions before agreeing to be in the study or afterward. The Informed Consent Form link is:

https://docs.google.com/file/d/0B48eSsYOuxOPeUstNjBpTDFyTDg/edit?usp=sharing

If you agree and accept the conditions of the study and return a signed Informed Consent Form, you will be given a second link to the surveys through email. Please respond honestly and completely. Submission of the completed surveys will conclude your participation in the study. Information regarding withdrawing from the study is included with the Informed Consent Form.

Your Unique Research PIN

Your unique, alphanumeric research PIN is: XXXXXX. Please do not disclose this PIN, which will be used to ensure confidentiality on your survey responses. If you wish to withdraw from the survey, your PIN will be used to locate your responses and withdraw them from the study.

Contact and Questions

Thank you for taking the time to consider participation in this study. If you have any questions now or at any time during the research study, I can be reached through email at sgalati1026@email.phoenix.edu or by telephone at 207-485-1901.

Sincerely,

Stephen R. Galati

University of Phoenix, Doctoral Student

APPENDIX G
CONFIDENTIALITY AGREEMENT

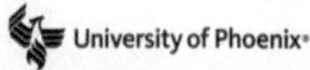

ENTERING THE GLOBAL ENGINEERING MARKET: A CORRELATIONAL STUDY OF CULTURAL INTELLIGENCE AND MARKET ORIENTATION
STEPHEN R. GALATI

CONFIDENTIALITY STATEMENT

As a researcher working on the above research study at the University of Phoenix, I understand that I must maintain the confidentiality of all information concerning all research participants as required by law. Only the University of Phoenix Institutional Review Board may have access to this information. "Confidential Information" of participants includes but is not limited to: names, characteristics, or other identifying information, questionnaire scores, ratings, incidental comments, other information accrued either directly or indirectly through contact with any participant, and/or any other information that by its nature would be considered confidential. In order to maintain the confidentiality of the information, I hereby agree to refrain from discussing or disclosing any Confidential Information regarding research participants, to any individual who is not part of the above research study or in need of the information for the expressed purposes on the research program. This includes having a conversation regarding the research project or its participants in a place where such a discussion might be overheard; or discussing any Confidential Information in a way that would allow an unauthorized person to associate (either correctly or incorrectly) an identity with such information. I further agree to store research records whether paper, electronic or otherwise in a secure locked location under my direct control or with appropriate safe guards. I hereby further agree that if I have to use the services of a third party to assist in the research study, who will potentially have access to any Confidential Information of participants, that I will enter into an agreement with said third party prior to using any of the services, which shall provide at a minimum the confidential obligations set forth herein. I agree that I will immediately report any known or suspected breach of this confidentiality statement regarding the above research project to the University of Phoenix, Institutional Review Board.

Signature	**Stephen R. Galati**	05/24/2013
Signature of Researcher	Printed Name	Date
Signature	**Janet Galati**	05/24/2013
Signature of Witness	Printed Name	Date

Current version 032012

ABOUT THE AUTHOR

Dr. Stephen Galati has more than 20 years of proposal management, technical writing, grant writing, marketing communications, training and training course development, and electrical engineering experience throughout the United States and for global opportunities. He is the author of Geographic Information Systems Demystified, a textbook published by Artech House, and has numerous publications to his credit concerning environmental consulting, proposal writing, grant management, and public / private funding. He holds a Doctor of Management degree in Organizational Leadership with the University of Phoenix, a Master's Degree in English Rhetoric from the City University of New York, a Bachelor's Degree in Electrical Engineering from Pratt Institute, and a Professional Development Certificate in Emergency Management from the FEMA Institute.

www.ingramcontent.com/pod-product-compliance
Lightning Source LLC
Chambersburg PA
CBHW020909180526
45163CB00007B/2676

*9 781545 387542 *